# *Maximizing Leadership Effectiveness*

Impact of
Administrative Style
on Faculty and Students

Alexander W. Astin

Rita A. Scherrei

# *Maximizing Leadership Effectiveness*

## Jossey-Bass Publishers

San Francisco • Washington • London • 1980

MAXIMIZING LEADERSHIP EFFECTIVENESS
*Impact of Administrative Style on Faculty and Students*
by Alexander W. Astin and Rita A. Scherrei

Copyright © 1980 by: Jossey-Bass Inc., Publishers
433 California Street
San Francisco, California 94104
&
Jossey-Bass Limited
28 Banner Street
London EC1Y 8QE

**Library of Congress Cataloging in Publication Data**

Astin, Alexander W
    Maximizing leadership effectiveness.

    Includes bibliographical references and index.
    1. Universities and colleges—United States—
Administration. 2. Leadership. 3. College
presidents—United States. I. Scherrei, Rita A.,
joint author. II. Title.
LB2341.A756        378.73        79-9665
ISBN 0-87589-454-2

Manufactured in the United States of America

JACKET DESIGN BY WILLI BAUM

FIRST EDITION

*Code 8017*

The Jossey-Bass
Series in Higher Education

# *Preface*

~~~~~~~~~~~~~~~~~~~~~~~~~~~~~~~~~~~~~~~~~~~~~~

The study reported here was conducted in connection with the Exxon Education Foundation's Resource Allocation Management Program (RAMP), a five-year program of grants awarded to some forty-nine private colleges and universities between 1972 and 1977. The evolution of the RAMP project is described in the first chapter of a related volume by Baldridge and Tierney (1979). While that book focuses on the implementation and use of computerized information systems and management by objectives in higher education, this one concentrates on administrative style and its effects on faculty and students. Its findings should be of general interest to the higher education community, but they are especially relevant to the concerns of current and would-be administrators, faculty, and those who recruit, select, and prepare academic administrators.

We undertook this study because we felt that administrative *outcomes* was the most neglected area in the literature on academic administration and that the RAMP programs provided an excellent opportunity to begin an exploration of this critical topic. If the way in which an institution is administered affects the quality of the education it offers, we felt it would be easiest to observe such relationships in a sample of private liberal arts colleges. We were, nevertheless, not particularly optimistic about being able to find many statistically significant relationships, given the relatively small size of the sample (forty-nine institutions) and given the widespread belief in academe that the president and other administrators really have little power and influence.

We were, to put it mildly, surprised by the results. Presidential and administrative styles *are* related to a number of faculty and student outcomes. Moreover, many of the relationships seem plausible and consistent with theory.

We have become acutely aware that drawing causal inferences about the effects of administrative styles on faculty and students is a risky business, at best. While the data on which this study is based are relatively comprehensive and in many ways unique, they fall short of what one would want in the ideal study design: longitudinal data on both faculty and students, background data on the presidents' administrative predispositions prior to coming to the institution, and a large sample of institutions. Perhaps the most difficult problem in this type of research is timing: The best designed study would be one where baseline (pretest) data on administrators, faculty, and students are collected from a sample of "experimental" institutions at the time a new president takes office. Subsequent behavioral changes, which would be assessed by means of follow-up (posttest) data, could then be examined in the experimental institutions and simultaneously in a matched sample of "control" institutions that do not change presidents during the same time period. Such a study, of course, would require considerably more time and resources than were available in the present study. If nothing else, we hope that the results of our study will prove to be sufficiently provocative to stimulate some funding agency to support such a study.

This research project was supported entirely by a grant from the Exxon Education Foundation to the Higher Education Research Institute. We are particularly appreciative of the advice, encouragement, and freedom of action provided by the Foundation staff: H. C. Roser, Jr. and Frederick deW. Bolman, who initially developed the idea for the RAMP project; Walter J. Kenworthy, who conceived the idea for a behavioral evaluation of the project; and Richard R. Johnson, who shared the task of overseeing the project.

We are indebted to a number of other people who contributed their time, energy, and creativity to this complex undertaking. Michele Harway and Lewis Solmon were chief collaborators in the early conceptual stages of the project, when we were designing the instrumentation and contacting the participating institutions. Norman Lynn Bailiff assisted at that point with valuable advice. The principal burden of planning and engineering the visits to the institutions was carried by Michele Harway and Michael Tierney, although they received invaluable help from many persons who were consultants or members of the various site visit teams: Marguerite Archie, George Beatty, Dennis Boos, David Bushnell, Craig Comstock, David Epperson, Ann Finkelstein Drew, Richard Gilman, John Hubbard, Joseph Katz, C. P. Kerley, Micki Lane, James March, Barbara S. McCaslin, John Minter, C. Robert Pace, Michele Patterson, Maurice Salter, Warren Schmidt, Jeanne M. Suhr, Mary Ruth Swint, Chuck Thomas, Beverly T. Watkins, James Welch, John Whiteley, Logan Wilson, and Jed Zaharchuk.

The early programming expertise of Leonard Woren and Gerald T. Richardson greatly facilitated the later data analyses. Preliminary secretarial work on the project was carried out by Mary Ruth Swint and Carol Feldman.

The very difficult task of reading and interpreting over 2,000 personal interviews with administrators and faculty was shared by David S. Webster, who also drafted important sections of

Appendix F. Laura Kent's editorial talents made the manuscript much more readable, despite the limited time she had to work on it. Louis T. Benezet helped us enormously with his detailed critique of the preliminary draft. The comments of Joseph Katz and J. Victor Baldridge were also appreciated.

Finally, we would like to express our appreciation to the hundreds of busy administrators, faculty, and students who contributed their time to this ambitious undertaking. We hope that we have been able to treat their responses with some care and sensitivity and that they or their successors will be able to benefit from the results.

*Los Angeles, California*                    ALEXANDER W. ASTIN
*March 1980*                                 RITA A. SCHERREI

# Contents

**xiii**

Resources

# The Authors

ALEXANDER W. ASTIN is professor of higher education at the University of California, Los Angeles (UCLA); president of the Higher Education Research Institute; and director of the Cooperative Institutional Research Program. Previously, he was director of research for the American Council on Education (1965-1973) and the National Merit Scholarship Corporation (1960-1964). His work has appeared in more than one hundred articles and twelve books, including *Four Critical Years* (Jossey-Bass, 1977), *Preventing Students from Dropping Out* (Jossey-Bass, 1975), and *The Power of Protest* (Jossey-Bass, 1975). Astin has received awards for outstanding research from the American Personnel and Guidance Association (1965), the National Association of Student Personnel Administrators (1976), and the American College Personnel Association (1978). He has also been a fellow at the Center for Advanced Study in the Behavioral Sciences at Stanford, California (1967-1968).

Astin received his doctor's and master's degrees in psychology from the University of Maryland and his bachelor's degree in music from Gettysburg College.

RITA A. SCHERREI is a research analyst at the Higher Education Research Institute. She is currently participating in a major study on the status of disadvantaged minorities in higher education and is pursuing her research interests on educational issues related to women and on the status of Catholic higher education. Recently she published a chapter in *New Directions for Education, Work, and Careers: Enhancing Women's Career Development* (Jossey-Bass, 1979, no. 8). Before becoming involved in educational research, Scherrei taught chemistry and mathematics in secondary schools and at the beginning college level and was a chemical reference librarian.

Her doctor's degree in higher education was awarded by UCLA (1980). Scherrei's other degrees include a master's in library science (UCLA) and in chemistry (Seattle University) and a bachelor's degree in chemistry (Mount St. Mary's College, Los Angeles).

# *Maximizing Leadership Effectiveness*

~~~~~~~~~~~~~~~~~~~~~~~~~~~~~~~~~~~~~~~~~~~~~~~~~~

## Impact of Administrative Style on Faculty and Students

# ONE

# *Assessing*
# *Administrative Impacts*

~~~~~~~~~~~~~~~~~~~~~~~~~~~~~~

The study reported in this book involved five years of intensive analysis of forty-nine private colleges and universities. It has focused on one major question: How does the institution's particular style of management and administration affect faculty and students? This first chapter shows how we have sought to answer this question and consists of three major parts: the rationale for the study, an overview of the literature on academic administration, and the design of the study.

## Rationale for the Study

Our research project derived in part from five basic assumptions about higher education administration:

1. The ultimate goal of administration in any organization is to facilitate the fulfillment of the aims of that organization. In

educational institutions, the measure of effectiveness is the maximization of faculty productivity and the enhancement of student learning and development.

2. In studying the process of college administration, the researcher must distinguish between administrative *behavior* and the educational *effectiveness* of that behavior on faculty and students.

3. The literature on college administration reviewed later in this chapter tends to view administrative behavior or the administrative process as an end in itself rather than as a means to realize educational ends. Thus, empirical research in the field has not produced very much information on the relationship between management and educational outcomes.

4. Academic administrators have traditionally been more concerned about the *acquisition* of resources (money, facilities, faculty, students) than about their effective *use*. Similarly, recent concerns about inflation, the "steady state," and declining enrollments in higher education have focused on how to conserve limited resources rather than on how to reallocate them for the enhancement of student and faculty development.

5. A critical need for research in higher education is to understand how various administrative behaviors and styles affect faculty and students.

This last premise constitutes the principal question addressed by the study reported in this book. Accordingly, we must first define more precisely the terms *educational outcome* and *administrative behavior*.

*Educational Outcomes of Administrative Behavior.* How does one assess the educational consequences of administrative actions? Perhaps the simplest way to approach this highly complex question is first to conceive of a continuum of possible outcomes. One end of the continuum includes those *proximate* outcomes most directly affected by administrative behavior; the *distal* end includes outcomes that are expected to bear only a very remote connection to administrative practices (see Table 1). For example, if the pres-

**Table 1. Examples of Administrative Variables and Their Possible Outcomes**

| | Examples of Possible | |
| --- | --- | --- |
| Administrative Variable | Proximate Outcomes | Distal Outcomes |
| 1. President behaves in autocratic manner | Other administrators perceive president as autocratic | Student attrition rate increases |
| 2. Size of counseling center staff is increased | Student satisfaction with counseling improves | Student vandalism decreases |
| 3. Faculty granted pay increase | Faculty morale improves | Student learning improves |

ident of an institution conducts his affairs in a very autocratic fashion (administrative behavior), one would expect that his closest associates would perceive him as autocratic. This perception is a relatively proximate outcome of an autocratic presidential style. A slightly less proximate outcome is the perception of the president by those who would be expected to have less direct contact with him (for example, students and faculty). A relatively distal outcome is the rate of student attrition.

Note that, in all the examples given in Table 1, the proximate outcomes involve attitudes. All three examples of distal outcomes, on the other hand, involve some aspect of student behavior. The table thus illustrates two principles of the outcome continuum: (1) Administrative behavior is likely to affect most directly attitudes (particularly attitudes about the administration); and (2) Administrative behavior is likely to only indirectly affect most student outcomes.

These two principles suggest a possible explanation of why treatises on administration generally ignore potential learning outcomes: The *apparent* connection between administrative practice and student learning is, at best, remote. But administrators generally recognize that their behavior directly affects how they are perceived by others (regardless of possible learning outcomes).

Indeed, the collective attitudes of faculty members toward the administration can cause administrators to lose their jobs. It is thus easy to see why many administrators are accused of being "political" rather than educational in their styles of operation: They would rather focus their efforts on those attitudinal outcomes that are easier to affect directly and that may determine whether they keep their jobs.

The preceding paragraph emphasizes the word *apparent* to underscore two points. First, since administrative behavior probably has a number of unintended effects on student outcomes, it is important to understand what some of these "side effects" are. Second, although the connection between administrative practice and student outcomes may appear remote, this does not necessarily imply that it always is or that it ought to be. On the contrary, one of the major policy conclusions from this study (see Chapter Eight) is that administrative practice in American higher education could be improved significantly if student outcomes were given a more central place in the planning and decision-making process.

*The Varieties of Administration.* Assuming that measures of different behavioral outcomes at various points on the continuum could be developed, the researcher must next determine whether different outcomes are associated with different types of administrations. How do administrations differ from one college to the next? Which of these differences are most likely to affect faculty and student outcomes? In certain respects, the problem of describing differences in college administrations is a taxonomic question: What are the varieties of administrators and administrative styles? Is there a set of mutually exclusive categories into which various college administrations can be sorted? Unfortunately, the literature on higher education administration is not very helpful in suggesting alternative taxonomies of college administrations. Instead, much of it either focuses on the stereotypic attributes of college administrations or simply dichotomizes administrative styles as autocratic and democratic.

In summary, the research described in this book comprises two major tasks: the description and classification of different types of college administrations and the analysis of how these different types of administrations affect different faculty and student outcomes.

## The Literature on Academic Administration

Rather than attempting a comprehensive review of the literature on higher education administration, we are highlighting a number of earlier studies that relate directly to some of the issues examined in this project. We first give a general overview of management theory and then discuss that portion of the literature on management in higher education which focuses on administrative behaviors and educational outcomes.

*General Overview of Management Theory.* As Drucker (1974) and others have pointed out, the need for theories of organization did not emerge until the latter part of the nineteenth century, when complex organizations like multiservice banks and railroads were growing and when the control of many companies was passing from families and partnerships to boards and management teams.

People who sought to improve the efficiency and productivity of America's defense industries during World War II raised the subject of management to prominence. Before the war, there were only two companies with management development programs, three university programs in continuing education for managers, and no more than sixty or seventy volumes on management (Drucker, 1974). The business schools were schools of commerce, finance, and accounting, not management. By contrast, today in-house management development programs, university-level continuing education classes, and management libraries flourish, and many former business schools have been renamed management schools to better reflect their current emphasis.

Although the works of the early organization theorists remained fairly obscure until after World War II, they laid the groundwork for one of the three major schools of management: scientific management. This classical approach contains both a theory of motivation and a theory of organization.

Stressing effectiveness and control, the motivation approach of Frederick Taylor (1912) is based on the analogy that, just as a machine's successful operation depends on the function of each part, so an organization's successful operation depends on each worker's task. Narrowly defined tasks, standardized procedures, and strictly delineated supervisorial chains characterize this approach. The Taylor school proposed that, to motivate workers, payment should be as closely tied to output as possible, in terms of time (hourly wages, for example, are better than daily wages), merit, and quality.

The classical organization theory presented by Gulick and Urwick (1937) rests on the premise that division of labor, whereby jobs are broken down and workers become highly skilled in specialized tasks, will result in high efficiency. Paralleling the division of labor, a unity of command, whereby each line supervisor controls a limited number of workers (or other second-line supervisors), is suggested. The resulting organization resembles a pyramid, with workers at the base and top executives at the apex. Within the pyramid, specializations or departments are organized according to one or more of the following principles: purpose of the task, process involved in the task, clientele served, and geographical location. In actuality, the lower levels tend to be organized by the latter two principles and the higher levels by the first two.

Max Weber, in his well-known treatise, *The Theory of Social and Economic Organization* (1947), sees organizations as bureaucracies run by rules and divided internally by functions. A hierarchical authority structure prevails, with positions defined separately from the individuals who might occupy them. There must be a rational commitment of those lower in rank to those higher and to the organization itself. The only nonbureaucratic member is the head, who may provide a warm image to reinforce the abstractions of norms, rules, and ranks.

By the 1950s, a growing reaction against the depersonalized approach of the classical school resulted in the rise of the humanistic or person-oriented school, in which the worker rather than the organization becomes the focus. The educational theories of John Dewey and the psychological theories of Kurt Lewin, as well as the famous Hawthorne Study, led to serious questioning of the direct relation between the individual worker and productivity.

Drucker (1950) and Herzberg (1959) discuss the complex intrinsic and extrinsic motivational factors that affect work. Humanistic psychologists such as Maslow (1954) emphasize that adults need to share the responsibility rather than to be cast into childlike, dependent roles in their work settings. In effect, the humanistic school maintains that the most satisfying organization is the most efficient, whereas the classical school assumes that the most efficient organization is the most satisfying. According to the first view, the social and psychological needs of employees are satisfied in order to ensure cooperation and efficiency; according to the second, efficiency results in higher productivity and the ensuing economic rewards satisfy workers.

McGregor (1960) summarizes the two theories by positing them as extreme choices. Either managers assume that their employees are incapable of taking responsibility and thus must be closely supervised and regulated, or they assume that their employees are inherently responsible and motivated to achieve and thus emphasize freedom and initiative. According to McGregor, the first assumption is effective when outputs are directly measurable and where intrinsic job satisfaction is limited. When personal involvement is required and outcomes are difficult to quantify, the second assumption is the better choice.

In the last fifteen years, a structuralist school, which suggests that neither extreme is the answer, has gained prominence (Argyris, 1960; Haire, 1964; March and Simon, 1958). March and Simon (1958) point out that—unlike the classical "economic man," who operates in a highly specific environment and makes decisions from a preexisting set of choices or rules—an actual manager operates with personal wants, motives, and drives accompanied by limited knowledge and limited capacity to solve ambiguous problems.

Etzioni (1964) summarizes the structuralist view that organizations are composed of groups which share some values and interests but at the same time necessarily differ on issues such as power and wages. While the humanist school emphasizes the supremacy of social rewards, and the classical school emphasizes the necessity of efficiency and hierarchical organization, both would agree that conflict within the organization is undesirable. The structuralists, on the other hand, see conflict not only as inherent in organizations but also as a catalyst for development and change.

In attempting to relate the three schools to the management and organization of higher education institutions, one should bear in mind that the classical and humanist authors turned their attention to academic organizations rather late. They had already spent three quarters of a century studying factories, banks, railroads, and other profit-making or governmental agencies. The structuralists, on the other hand, include in their purview such nonprofit and semiprofessional organizations as hospitals, social work agencies, and schools.

The literature on organizational theory as applied to higher education reflects twin interests. Much of it focuses on the structural aspects (diffuse goals, professional technology, fragmentation into interest groups) or decision models (political, bureaucratic, collegial). There is, however, a large block of material on leadership style, especially the behavior of presidents.

As Baldridge and others (1978) point out, colleges and universities differ in many respects from corporations, factories, and government offices. Their goals are diffuse and ambiguous, in contrast to the rather clear objectives of a business (Cohen and March, 1974). The personnel consist of professionals who often identify more closely with the disciplines they represent than with the institutions. These professionals act autonomously in many respects; they do not fit classical descriptions of workers or humanistic descriptions of social participants.

At the same time, academic institutions employ a corps of nonprofessional or quasi-professional middle managers who are responsible for noninstructional services and who have fairly sizable staffs. These managers and their staffs often conform to a bureaucratic model of organization as they coexist with the professionals in the academic community.

Some theoreticians attempt to describe the entire organizational structure of the college or university in almost pure or classical terms (Stroup, 1966). Others attempt what can be termed an extreme humanistic approach, that of collegial management (Goodman, 1962; Millett, 1962). Neither, apparently, is satisfactory (Baldridge and others, 1978). The structuralists admit that elements of both views can be properly applied to different aspects of college management. In addition, however, they cite the ongoing conflicts among various pressure groups both within and outside the organization that lead to compromise and change; they conclude that a political model more closely resembles this process than a linear, rational decision-making model does.

With these three models in mind, our study focused on presidential and total administrative styles and their ripple effects upon the principal academic consumers, the faculty and the students. We hypothesized that, in smaller liberal arts colleges, the president and chief administrators do affect the organizational model dominating the college. That is, some institutions will closely resemble a bureaucratic model, others a collegial model, and others a structuralist or political model. Part of the resemblance, at least, will result from the style of the leaders, which in turn will affect the attitudes, behavior, and overall satisfaction of faculty and students.

*Specific Literature on Academic Administration and Educational Outcomes.* Precedence for this leadership approach can be found in several studies. On the basis of data from 115 American colleges and universities, Blau (1973) states: "The personal qualities of the president can decisively influence the fate of an academic institution . . . and they have much to do with how he exercises his authority and how much authority he has to exercise" (p. 179). Blau's study relates the performance of students and faculty to administrative structure, in particular to the extent of bureaucratization. Using indicators of this bureaucratization as independent variables, controlling for several other institutional characteristics, and using measures of the scholarship of students and faculty as dependent variables, Blau shows that such relationships exist. He concludes that, because a bureaucratic administrative structure distances the president and other administrators from students and faculty, it impedes communication and interferes with the integration of the scholarly enterprise. As a result, the rates at which students complete their degrees and graduates go on to graduate school decline. A bureaucratic structure also has detrimental effects on teaching but not, apparently, on research.

Sanders (1973) argues that the university community comprises faculty, administrative, and student networks. He claims that interaction between faculty and administration varies with the president's behavior as it is expressed in democratic or in autocratic decision making. Similarly, he believes that students, at least through their elected or self-appointed representatives, can interact with the administration to create either an antagonistic or a cooperative campus environment.

Hodgkinson (1970) analyzes presidential styles using data from 900 interviews with students, administrators, and department chairmen at nineteen colleges and universities. His study focuses on how and with whom the chief executive consults, delegates, and channels information. He concludes that more complex styles than simply the dichotomous autocratic and democratic exist; for instance, some hierarchical presidents delegate and consult openly, others consult secretively, and still others refuse to share decision making. Conversely, some democratic presidents decentralize but maintain responsibility for resolving conflict and maintaining lines of communication, others decentralize to the point of ambiguity, and—at the extreme—a few presidents preside with no power center in what Hodgkinson sees as a style approaching anarchy.

A five-zone model of administrative influence is postulated in the report of a task force convened jointly by the American Association of Higher Education and the National Education Association (1967). Placed along a continuum are administrative dominance, administrative primacy, shared authority, faculty primacy, and faculty dominance. After examining interview data from twenty-eight public and six private colleges and universities in which some major faculty-administration development was occurring, the task force concludes that about half the institutions could be placed in the administrative primacy zone, a quarter in the shared authority zone, and most of the remainder in the administrative dominance zone. Finally, the task force notes that faculty discontent is closely related to their lacking influence in governance.

The sample of institutions in the present study consists of private colleges, most of them fairly small. According to higher education folklore, buttressed by arguments presented in Goodman (1962) and Millett (1962), small colleges are havens of shared authority or collegiality. But studies by Blau (1973) and by Baldridge and others (1973) conclude that large schools apparently provide more opportunities for faculty participation in academic decision making and for autonomy in professional work. These latter researchers conclude that only a few of the small elite institutions are models of collegiality in Millett's sense of the word.

This book builds on these organizational theories of academic management. We first identify the dominant *presidential leadership styles* (Chapter Three). Next, we explore more general patterns of *administrative style* (Chapter Four). Finally, we discuss how leadership and administrative style affect the institution's culture, morale, faculty, and students (Chapters Five and Six). In many ways this approach follows that of Burton Clark (1970) in studying the relationship of institutional leadership to institutional "sagas," although he uses case studies while we use quantitative survey data.

We see our work as building on the foundations that other theorists such as Clark have furnished. We believe our special contribution, however, is the last step: linking presidential style and administrative patterns to student and faculty outcomes. Clearly, as the studies reviewed here show, distinct presidential styles and administrative environments exist and can be measured. They roughly parallel the classical and humanistic organization models as well as the more complex overlap of the two which represents the structuralist or political model. Moreover, some evidence suggests that student and faculty outcomes are affected by the styles which predominate on a campus. In 1971 Burton Clark suggested, in speaking of organizational sagas, that "we perhaps in the end can even link matters of governance to the quality of life within the modern college" (1971, p. 515). This study attempts to accomplish such a linkage.

## Design of the Study

Our study was designed as an adjunct to a major program of institutional grants carried out by the Exxon Education Foundation between 1972 and 1977. This grant program, called the Resource Allocation Management Program (RAMP), was intended to help liberal arts colleges improve their management systems. Private institutions across the country were challenged to submit proposals for introducing modern management practices to their campuses. The RAMP projects on each campus are analyzed in a recent report by Baldridge and Tierney (1979).

The RAMP program provided us with an ideal opportunity to engage in an intensive analysis of the administrations on each of the recipient campuses. Accordingly, each campus was visited by a team of researchers from the Higher Education Research Institute (HERI); they interviewed members of the administration, faculty, and student body, asked these groups to complete self-administered questionnaires, and collected other information about the institutional environment.

*The Institutional Sample.* Forty-seven of the forty-nine institutions were visited by the HERI research teams between spring 1974 and spring 1977. This extended period of initial data collection was necessitated by the fact that the Exxon Education Foundation allocated its grant awards over a four-year interval. Questionnaires were again administered to faculty, students, and administrators at a subsample of forty of these institutions in spring 1977. An average of twenty months elapsed between the initial and the follow-up data collection efforts. It was not possible to collect follow-up questionnaires from the remaining institutions because their initial grant awards were made too late in the project.

Although the RAMP grants were limited to private institutions, the sample is diverse with respect to a number of potentially important characteristics. The median enrollment is between 1,500 and 2,000 students, with a range from 250 to 10,000. The mean selectivity scores (total of SAT Verbal and Mathematical scores of entering freshmen) are 1,000 to 1,074, with a high of above 1,300 and a low of less than 775. Six of the institutions are Roman Catholic, fifteen are affiliated with a Protestant denomination, and twenty-six are nonsectarian. With the exception of four universities and four technological institutions, the sample consists of liberal arts colleges. Five of the institutions have predominantly black student bodies. All geographical regions are represented: nineteen of the institutions are located in the Northeast, six in the South, fourteen in the Midwest, and eight in the Far West and Southwest.

*Administrative Data.* Given that most higher educational institutions have similar formal administrative structures, the singular characteristics of any given institution's administration are determined to a substantial degree by the particular people occupying the top administrative posts. The principal administrators of these institutions ordinarily include: the chief executive officer (president or chancellor), the chief academic officer, the chief fiscal officer, the chief student affairs officer, the chief planning or development officer, the director of admissions, the registrar, and the director of financial aid.

Three methods were used to collect information about each of these administrators on each campus: personal interviews, self-administered questionnaires, and informants. In the personal interviews, the administrator was asked to describe his or her major responsibilities, decision-making style, major accomplishments, disappointments and frustrations, and plans for the future. Administrators other than the president were also asked to comment on the president's style of operation and its principal effects on the institution. (The questions asked during the chief academic officer's personal interview are listed in Appendix A.)

The self-administered questionnaires contain a number of items designed to assess the administrator's typical behavior patterns: frequency of personal contact with other administrators, faculty, students, and others; favored means of communication (through staff, memoranda, telephone calls, personal conversations, formal meetings, and so on); sources relied upon for information about the administration (meetings, personal conversations, memoranda, gossip, and so on); and time devoted to campus and off-campus activities. Administrators were also asked to indicate their perceptions of which administrative traits (aggressiveness, creativity, interpersonal skills, and so forth) are rewarded at their institutions; how they reward their own subordinates; their opinions about the institution's weakest and strongest qualities; and their degree of satisfaction with various aspects of their job (salary, status, autonomy, and so forth). (The questionnaire for the chief academic officer is reproduced in Appendix B.)

*Faculty Data.* We obtained information from faculty through personal interviews and self-administered questionnaires. Since we did not have sufficient resources to interview all faculty members, we asked each RAMP project director to select at random one faculty member from each major curricular area (social science, natural science, arts, humanities, and professional schools). An average of four to five such interviews were conducted on each campus. During the interviews, faculty were asked to comment on the decision-making process at the departmental level (including adequacy of faculty input), adequacy of faculty input into higher-level decisions, adequacy of information concerning administrative practices, perceptions of the president's style of governance, major obstacles or frustrations, and major assets of being a faculty member at the institution. (The faculty questionnaire is reproduced in Appendix C.)

The self-administered questionnaires elicit the faculty members' opinions on matters such as the quality of support services (typing, research assistants, and so forth), the degree of input to the administration, and the quality of administrative decision making at the institution. A similar but somewhat expanded questionnaire was used for departmental chairpersons to assess items such as the following: percentage of time spent in various activities, communication patterns with other administrators and with departmental colleagues, autonomy in developing departmental budgets, accounting procedures, purchasing procedures, record keeping, and satisfaction with various aspects of the chairperson's position.

Because department chairpersons are intermediaries between the faculty and the administration, one of the site visit team members met with them in a group to discuss matters such as the following: importance and influence of various faculty committees on institutional policy, methods for determining departmental budgets, input into higher-level administrative decision-making processes, adequacy of information about administrative policies and decisions, adequacy of student involvement in decision making, quality of student-faculty interaction, and effectiveness of the advising system.

*Student Data.* We obtained information from students through self-administered questionnaires and a group interview with a sample of student leaders such as the student body president, editor of the campus paper, and heads of various major student organizations. The group interview with students covered such general issues as: student involvement in administrative decisions, the quality of the educational program, the extent to which rules and regulations about personal behavior are enforced, and overall satisfaction with the college.

The self-administered student questionnaire covers factors

such as involvement in student organizations, use of various student services (financial aid, career counseling, housing, and so on), satisfaction with student services, and perceptions of the administration. We collected questionnaires from at least twenty-five students on each campus. (The student questionnaire is reproduced in Appendix D.)

Additional longitudinal student data for special analyses of the relationship between administrative style and student attrition were obtained from the files of the Cooperative Institutional Research Program (CIRP). These files and the method of analysis used to study attrition are described in Chapter Six.

*Data Analyses.* In analyzing these extensive data, we had two major objectives: to develop a taxonomy of college administrations and to assess the impact of different types of administrations on student and faculty outcomes.

The development of a taxonomy of college administrations involves a series of correlational and factor analyses of the questionnaire and interview data from administrators and faculty. Results of these analyses are reported in Chapters Two (profiles of chief administrators), Three (presidential styles), and Four (varieties of college administrations).

The impact of administrative styles on faculty and student outcomes is analyzed within the framework of the descriptive taxonomies presented in Chapters Three and Four; these taxonomies constitute the independent variables, and the faculty and student data are the dependent variables. For those institutions whose student and faculty outcomes we assessed on a pretest-posttest longitudinal basis, we were able to investigate the effect of administrative styles on *changes* in student and faculty outcomes. These longitudinal analyses, however, generally prove to be disappointing because we obtained usable follow-up data from only a very small number of institutions. Accordingly, in order to take advantage of the largest possible sample size, we rely almost exclusively on cross-sectional analyses of pretest data in subsequent chapters.

We must emphasize that these analyses are only suggestive of possible causal connections between administrative behaviors and student or faculty outcomes since the cross-sectional research design falls far short of a classical control group experiment. Even if we had adequate data for longitudinal analyses, any negative results would be difficult to interpret since administrative variables may have had their effects prior to the pretest measurement of student and faculty outcomes.

Another problem in making causal interpretations from analyses of the relationships between administrative variables and student or faculty outcomes is the possibility that other, uncontrolled characteristics of institutions may mediate these relations. Highly selective colleges, for example, may tend to have certain types of administrations and, at the same time, to have certain effects on student development independent of the administration. In these circumstances, the failure to control for the selectivity of the college would yield a spurious relationship between administrative and student outcome variables. To minimize the possibility of such spurious effects, our analyses control simultaneously for several institutional attributes: selectivity, race, sex, affluence, size, control (Protestant, Roman Catholic, nonsectarian), and geographical region. Several other variables such as the population of the town in which the college is located, the percentage of students in residence, and the relative urbanity of the town's location are also included in the analyses. These control variables were obtained from the Higher Education General Information Survey data (1973), Cass and Birnbaum's *Comparative Guide to American Colleges* (1973), *Lovejoy's College Guide* (1976), the *Hammond World Atlas* (1974), and the colleges' own published catalogues.

What, then, do we have to say about the validity of the results reported here? Do our findings constitute convincing evidence of a causal link between administrative practices and student and faculty outcomes? While each reader will decide this question on the basis of the evidence presented, we would like to share briefly our own views about this study.

Perhaps the major difficulty with any correlational study is that the results are necessarily ambiguous. Take, for example, our finding that a bureaucratic president and a hierarchical administration are associated with student dissatisfaction, particularly with administrative services (Chapter Six). Aside from the obvious inference that this type of administration is less able to respond to student needs because it is too removed from the students and from those lower-level staff members who deal directly with students, this finding is subject to several alternative explanations: Could it be that certain types of institutions (for example, relatively large and complex ones) are prone to hire bureaucratic presidents and less able to deliver adequate administrative services to students? Do large institutions with hierarchical administrations recruit bureaucratic presidents, or does the bureaucratic president encourage the development of a hierarchical style of administrative organization? Or could it be that new presidents fall into a bureaucratic style once they find themselves confronted by a hierarchical organization?

In trying to resolve such ambiguities, readers are encouraged to keep in mind the full weight of our analyses. For example, the interpretation that poor student services are in fact a consequence of bureaucratic presidents and hierarchical administrators gains some credence from the special analyses of the effects of the administration on student attrition (Chapter Six) and earlier research showing a direct link between student satisfaction and attrition (see Astin, 1977b). Similarly, the alternative explanation involving institutional size is not supported by two other lines of evidence: the relationship between a bureaucratic president and student dissatisfaction does not disappear entirely when size is controlled, and a bureaucratic style is more strongly associated with attrition than is institutional size. The weight of the evidence, however, is less clear with respect to the causal issue of how bureaucratic presidents come to be associated with hierarchical administrations. Are they hired by institutions that already have such administrations? Do they become bureaucratic only after confronting a hierarchical administration? Or does the bureaucratic president encourage the development of a hierarchical administration? Such ambiguities can only be resolved through additional research.

Results of the analyses of the effects of administrative variables are presented for faculty outcomes in Chapter Five and for student outcomes in Chapter Six. Chapter Seven summarizes the major empirical findings and discusses the practical implications that the major findings have for administrative practice. Chapter Eight presents our best ideas about how college administrations can more effectively serve the educational mission of their institutions. The Resources—Appendices A through F—include interview and questionnaire items that researchers and institutional self-study teams may wish to use or adapt in their own work.

# TWO

# *Profiles*
# *of Senior*
# *Academic Officers*

~~~~~~~~~~~~~~~~~~~~~~~~~~~~~~~

To provide a backdrop for the different presidential and general administrative styles to be presented in Chapters Three and Four, this chapter summarizes the questionnaire responses and interview data of 299 administrators at the forty-five institutions from which we received questionnaire data. On the assumption that the president has the greatest single effect on the organizational climate of an academic institution, presidents are considered separately. The questionnaire responses of other administrators are summarized into average institutional replies. For purposes of comparison, however, both groups are included in some of the tables.

## The Presidents

Because not all the presidents from the RAMP institutions responded to the survey questionnaire or participated in the interviews, the material discussed here is drawn from a sample of thirty-three presidents who completed questionnaires and twenty-three who were interviewed. Of the group of thirty-three, all but two are men; their average age is fifty-one years. Twenty-six of these chief executive officers hold doctorates, and a third of them have taught undergraduates within the three years prior to the survey. Close to half (45 percent) report that they have outside incomes of at least $5,000 a year. They report spending about 70 percent of their working time on campus, and the rest away on business or at meetings.

## Highlights and Disappointments

Some of the most revealing information provided by the college presidents themselves comes from their answers to the opening question from the personal interview: "Being president of a liberal arts college is a complex job that must involve many rewarding experiences as well as many frustrations. What do you consider one of the highlights of your presidency so far at this college? What has been one of your major disappointments?" An analysis of the presidents' diverse responses to this question suggests at least eight different categories into which their answers can be classified: general governance and administration, faculty, academic matters, fiscal matters, facilities, students, outside community, and personnel. The frequency with which the presidents spontaneously mentioned each of these areas is shown in Table 2. Approximately 10 percent of the 132 responses are classifiable in more than one category. Since presidents mention some categories (for example, students) with surprising infrequency, such responses were placed in the less frequently mentioned category. Thus, a response mentioning both faculty and students is reported in the student category.

Table 2. Highlights and Disappointments of the Presidents' Administrations (N = 23 presidents)

| Response Category | Number of Times Mentioned[a] | | |
|---|---|---|---|
| | Highlight | Disappointment | Total |
| General governance and administration | 19 | 13 | 32 |
| Faculty | 6 | 16 | 22 |
| Academic matters | 11 | 6 | 17 |
| Fiscal matters | 9 | 6 | 15 |
| Facilities | 8 | 3 | 11 |
| Students | 6 | 3 | 9 |
| Outside community | 8 | 0 | 8 |
| Personnel | 3 | 5 | 8 |
| Unclassified | 6 | 4 | 10 |
| Total | (76) | (56) | (132) |

[a]Open-ended responses to the question, "Being president of a liberal arts college is a complex job that must involve many rewarding experiences as well as many frustrations. What do you consider one of the highlights of your presidency so far at this college? What has been one of your major disappointments?"

Results for each of the eight categories are discussed separately below.

*General Governance and Administration.* Matters relating to general governance and administration are more frequently mentioned as highlights than as disappointments, although the presidents are generally more inclined to mention highlights (76) than disappointments (56). The types of responses given as highlights also differ somewhat from the disappointments. For example, about a third of the highlights in this category concern structural changes that have been introduced during the president's administration: change from single-sex to coeducation status, adoption of a 4-1-4 calendar, and introduction of a three-year degree program. None of the disappointments mention such structural changes (or a failure to implement them). The other administrative highlights also tend to be very explicit and concrete: for example, introduction of an administrative term of office, resolution of a collective bargaining contract, regional accreditation, development of a management system, and increased faculty and student involvement in decision making.

Many of the disappointments, by contrast, reflect more general matters relating to the administrative *process*; the following statements are representative:

• Not able to do everything I want.
• Communication gets perverted.
• They wait for the leader to make decisions.
• The whole process moves more slowly than it should.
• Doing other people's jobs takes time—bailing people out.
• The inability to promote and communicate some of the ideas and ideals I personally feel should exist.

Apparently, presidents are inclined to look at their successes in terms of specific accomplishments and at their failures in terms of the processes that prevented them from carrying out their plans. One may speculate about this pattern: Is it possible that presidents tend to take their successes for granted? Could some presidents become more effective managers if they focused more attention on the *processes* that lead to successful implementation of plans and ideas?

*Faculty.* Faculty are clearly the most frequent source of disappointment for college presidents; by contrast, faculty rank fifth in the list of highlights. This is consistent with Peterson's (1975) study of self-reported critical incidents for both new and experienced college presidents. He reports, for example, that one experienced president "quite bluntly labeled his faculty as childish and petty " (p. 49). Similarly, the presidents in our sample display a good deal of strong affect in expressing their disappointments about faculty. Presidents complain that some faculty are unable to accommodate change and be imaginative, that faculty are not understanding and supportive, that it is difficult to establish a relationship of mutual trust with the faculty, and that some faculty are suspect of the administration.

Interestingly enough, on the few occasions when presidents

mention faculty in connection with administrative highlights, they focus on a somewhat different aspect of the faculty's role in the institution; they comment on the restoration of faculty morale, the high quality of faculty, and their positive accomplishments in working with faculty.

With the possible exception of this last response, the presidents tend to view as their positive experiences with faculty those situations in which they helped or improved the faculty. Not a single president cites the faculty's helpfulness, positive contributions to the decision-making process, or general contribution to the institution. In other words, when presidents think of faculty as participants in the operation of the institution, they almost always see them in a negative light.

*Academic Matters.* Academic matters place second on the presidents' list of highlights, and are tied for third on the disappointment list. Academic highlights include general and specific achievements; for example, the introduction of a freshman humanities course, interdisciplinary study programs, revised curriculums, and increased academic quality.

Academic disappointments, on the other hand, focus mainly on the presidents' failure to devote sufficient energy to this important area. Several presidents regret that fiscal activities command so much of their attention; one said: "If I can devote 1 percent of my time to being an academic leader, I am lucky." Only one response—about the failure of a liberal arts seminar for business and professional people—touches on any specific academic program or policy. Given the obvious intensity of their concern about neglecting academic matters, one wonders why these presidents cannot find time or avenues of access which would enable them to become involved in this critical area. Because involvement in academic matters necessitates working with faculty, could it be that some presidents avoid such involvement simply to avoid conflict with faculty? Does preoccupation with fund raising and other fiscal matters provide a socially acceptable means for presidents to avoid this conflict-laden area of academic affairs?

*Fiscal Matters.* Fiscal matters occupy third place among both highlights and disappointments. Once again, however, comments about the highlights differ substantially in tone from comments about the disappointments. Typical fiscal highlights include substantial increases in the budget, successful fund-raising campaigns, and annual net surpluses. In contrast, the presidents express their disappointments more vaguely, in statements like: "There are financial things which make for a lot of frustrations"; "We don't have the ability to monitor the institution's budget with a high degree of accuracy"; "Failure to get a hold on the financial side"; and simply "Not enough money."

Considering the financial difficulties that many private institutions were experiencing during the years when these interviews were conducted (1974–1977), it is surprising that only six presidents mention financial matters as one of their major disappointments. Indeed among those who do mention finances, only one president refers to a lack of resources, whereas most of the rest express concerns about matters of fiscal control and budgeting. Either the financial plight of private institutions during this period has been greatly exaggerated, or many of these presidents prefer to disassociate themselves from these basic fiscal problems.

*Facilities.* Facilities are mentioned as highlights much more often than as failures. Typical examples of facilities highlights include new buildings, recreation areas, and an improved physical plant. Disappointments include insufficient facilities and the failure to construct new buildings.

*Students.* Although most of these presidents preside over undergraduate liberal arts colleges, student issues are far down the list of highlights (sixth) and disappointments (seventh). Clearly, students do not occupy a prominent place in the concerns of these liberal arts college presidents. Examples of student highlights are: the excellence of student body, alumni satisfaction, and the placement record of graduates.

Three presidents mention disappointments relating to students: that the quality of the student body has not been maintained; that students feel that since the college is not well known, something must be wrong with the college; and that there is fric-tion between faculty and students.

*Outside Community.* Responses concerning the college's rela-tions with the outside community produce the biggest discrepancy between highlights and disappointments. Outside community rela-tions place fourth in the list of presidents' highlights but are totally absent from the list of disappointments. Apparently, presidents either have no problems in their relations with outside constituen-cies or are simply unwilling to take any responsibility for failures in this area. Highlights in this category cover a wide range of issues: better relations between the institution and the city, regional im-pact and involvement, support from alumni and parents, and in-creased involvement in the community, including using the re-sources of the institution to solve the problems of the community.

These responses refer to two complementary processes: the college's greater involvement with and positive contribution to the community, and the greater acceptance of the college by outside constituencies.

*Personnel.* Responses are classified under this category if they focus on matters of recruitment or on issues relating to the quality of the performance of personnel (excluding faculty). The com-ments of the three presidents who mention personnel highlights are: "Bringing [name of administrator] here"; "Pleased with my management team"; and "Recruited outstanding personnel." Per-sonnel disappointments include the following comments: "Some people are not team players"; "Two or three staff members didn't pan out"; "Failure to get more women onto the faculty and staff"; and "Decline in the number of Jesuits available."

*Unclassifiable Responses.* Examples of miscellaneous highlights are: "The grant allowed us to continue to innovate"; "To return to the place that gave you your momentum"; and "To encourage the kind of change that needs to take place in higher education." The unclassifiable disappointments are: "I wish the regional consortium was doing more"; "The university is not very innovative"; "I feel lonely and isolated—my contacts are formal"; and "The job is no fun any more."

These last two responses may reflect the attitudes of more than just two college presidents. Indeed, the disappointments listed under academic matters and fiscal matters suggest that quite a few of these presidents are generally disappointed because they are not expected to function nor can they act as academic leaders in the manner they anticipated.

*Perceived Institutional Strengths and Weaknesses.* When asked to indicate the strong qualities of their institutions on the questionnaire, the presidents most frequently cite quality of teaching, overall institutional reputation, and the impact of the institution on students' academic development (see Table 3). The first and last mentioned strengths are consistent with interview data (reported later in this section) which suggest that these presidents view their colleges as teaching institutions. Institutional reputation is probably cited for a variety of reasons: Some of the colleges in the sample are fairly selective, others are the only college in their im-

**Table 3. Institutional Qualities Noted Most Often as Strengths by Presidents and Other Administrators (N = 33 presidents, 266 administrators)**

| Quality | Percentage Who Noted Quality as Strength | |
|---|---|---|
| | Presidents | Other Administrators |
| Quality of teaching | 60 | 54 |
| Overall institutional reputation | 47 | 55 |
| Institutional impact on students' academic development | 30 | 18 |
| Institutional impact on students' personal or character development | 23 | 19 |
| Scope of curricular programs | 17 | 19 |
| Financial soundness | 13 | 22 |

*Note:* See Appendix B for the list of seventeen items which these administrators were asked to evaluate as strengths or weaknesses of their institutions.

mediate geographical area, and still others are unique either in program offerings or in religious affiliation.

In their questionnaire responses, the presidents most frequently mention the following qualities as being in need of strengthening or improvement: financial soundness, alumni support, and faculty morale (see Table 4). That the presidents believe that alumni support needs strengthening is probably accounted for by their perception that the alumni are potential, but not yet sufficiently tapped, sources of financial support (as is indicated by the findings discussed in the section on predictions of change). Presidents mention two other weaknesses—financial soundness and faculty morale—as the areas of their most difficult decisions and biggest disappointments. Indeed, presidents comment on their negative relationships with and perceptions of the faculty often enough to render suspect any generalization that small colleges necessarily foster collegiality.

It seems somewhat curious that the presidents name the quality of teaching as an institutional strength and yet are critical of the faculty in other contexts, some of which were presented in the last section. As another illustration, in response to the open-ended interview question "When you look at your academic program

Table 4. Institutional Qualities Noted Most Often as Weaknesses by Presidents and Other Administrators

|  | Percentage Who Noted Quality as Weakness | |
| --- | --- | --- |
| Quality | Presidents | Other Administrators |
| Financial soundness | 43 | 52 |
| Alumni support | 39 | 38 |
| Faculty morale | 32 | 31 |
| Institutional impact on students' personal or character development | 25 | 22 |
| Overall institutional reputation | 25 | 18 |
| Scholarly accomplishment of faculty (research) | 21 | 17 |

(courses for credit), what aspect seems most beneficial to students?" one president replied: "The quality of the faculty and the fact that most of them are concerned about teaching undergraduate students." But later he said that the faculty was "not willing to adjust to the particular needs of minority students. . . . The slowness of the faculty to change is one frustrating thing." Another president praises the faculty for their ability to work with students on an individual basis and to develop fresh approaches to learning. He further comments on their strong commitment to undergraduate education. But he also says that "The faculty behave in an immature way, . . . are a serious frustration, . . . a serious obstacle. Faculty can wreak havoc." Yet another says that the most beneficial aspect of the academic program is "an able faculty interested in teaching first and foremost." The same president also states, however, that the attitude of the faculty is "a general disappointment. . . . We're not nearly as compatible as I'd like."

There are several plausible explanations for this tendency to commend the faculty as classroom teachers but to denigrate them as participants in the wider campus life and as human beings. First, it is likely that faculty members at these small liberal arts colleges are hired primarily for their teaching interests and skills, however subjectively these may be judged, rather than for any other qualities they may have. Second, faculty members—unlike other members of the college community—may be tenured and thus may have considerably more leeway in their behavior than do others; their freedom can cause problems for the president. Third, the same qualities that make an effective teacher—irreverence toward received ideas, a critical attitude toward accepted views, and a penchant for seeing many different sides of the same question—may make a person an abrasive and irritating colleague. Whatever the explanation, the presidents' ambivalent attitude toward faculty warrants further research.

*Predictions of Change.* In view of their concerns about financial soundness, it is striking that—when asked on the questionnaire for their predictions of change over the next five years—87 percent of the presidents anticipate increased budgets; 97 percent, in-

creases in revenue from alumni; 67 percent, increases from other
private sources; 60 percent, increases in support from corporations; and 50 percent, increases from the state (see Table 5). Only
from the federal government did more than half (62 percent) predict either declining support or the same level of support. Clearly,
despite their expressed anxieties over budgets, these surprisingly
optimistic presidents see income increasing on several fronts. This
finding is supported by Bowen and Minter (1976), who report virtually the same phenomenon.

In addition, though more than a third foresee decreases in
building projects, most of the presidents (53 percent) assume no
change in this area. Most also look forward either to no change or
to increases in student applicants (87 percent) and enrollments (83
percent).

**Table 5. Predictions About Institutional Changes**

|  | Percentage Predicting Probable Increases | |
| --- | --- | --- |
| Suggested Changes | Presidents | Other Administrators |
| Contributions from alumni | 96.7 | 84.9 |
| Size of total institutional budget | 86.7 | 83.7 |
| Private gifts | 66.7 | 80.2 |
| Corporate gifts | 60.0 | 72.1 |
| Proportion of tenured faculty | 43.3 | 32.9 |
| State funding | 50.0 | 52.4 |
| Federal funding | 37.9 | 36.0 |
| Involvement of board of trustees | 36.7 | 53.5 |
| Number of student applicants | 33.3 | 38.4 |
| Student enrollments | 31.0 | 37.6 |
| Quality of student applicants | 20.7 | 16.3 |
| Variety of possible majors | 17.2 | 27.1 |
| Externally funded research activity | 17.2 | 24.7 |
| Noneducational or auxiliary enterprises | 16.7 | 26.7 |
| Discretionary money | 16.7 | 49.4 |
| Size of administrative staff | 13.8 | 19.8 |
| Size of faculty | 10.3 | 23.5 |
| Building projects | 10.0 | 25.0 |
| Number of new faculty positions | 10.0 | 20.0 |

In other areas, their predictions are closer to what one might expect. Nine in ten anticipate either decreases or no change in the number of new faculty; 97 percent believe that the number of tenured faculty will either increase or remain at the same level. And most presidents expect little or no change in such areas as discretionary money, student quality, variety of majors, externally funded research, noneducational enterprises, and involvement of trustees.

## Patterns of Communication

Some of the most interesting evidence of presidential diversity is provided by the self-administered questionnaire. One section of this instrument contains a list of seventeen different members of the academic community, preceded by the following question: "In performing the duties of your office, how frequently do you have *personal* contact (including telephone conversations) with the following persons or categories of persons?" For each of the seventeen people or groups, the presidents were requested to select one of the following frequencies: several times daily, about once a day, several times each week, about once a week, monthly, and less than monthly. Table 6 shows how frequently the forty-four presidents report communicating with each of the seventeen people or groups, which are listed in order, from those having most frequent to those having least frequent communication with the president. Not surprisingly, the typical president communicates most frequently with his or her immediate staff: 84 percent of the presidents communicate personally with their staff members at least once a day. Most presidents also communicate on a daily basis with two other individuals: the chief academic officer and the chief fiscal officer. These data suggest that most college presidents have an inner circle of coworkers comprising the chief academic and fiscal officers and the president's immediate staff.

Since only one president in four reports communicating on a daily basis with the chief student affairs officer, here is additional evidence that this administrator is typically not as close to the president as are the chief fiscal and academic officers. This statistic also supports the hypothesis that student concerns are not high on most

Table 6. Frequency of President's Personal Conversations with Others
(N = 44 presidents)

| Person(s) Conversed With | Percentage of Presidents Who Converse at Least | | |
|---|---|---|---|
| | Daily | Several Times a Week | Once a Month |
| Immediate staff | 84 | 100 | 100 |
| Chief academic officer | 77 | 100 | 100 |
| Chief fiscal officer | 61 | 100 | 100 |
| Chief student affairs officer | 25 | 98 | 100 |
| Students | 21 | 93 | 93 |
| Visitors | 18 | 84 | 97 |
| Other academic administrators[a] | 11 | 95 | 97 |
| Other administrators[a] | 11 | 80 | 95 |
| Faculty | 11 | 71 | 93 |
| Potential donors | 9 | 84 | 100 |
| Potential students | 5 | 11 | 57 |
| Admissions officer | 2 | 80 | 100 |
| Financial aid officer | 0 | 30 | 84 |
| Registrar | 0 | 23 | 84 |
| Department chairpersons (collectively) | 0 | 5 | 23 |
| Outside consultants | 0 | 5 | 21 |

[a]Other than those specifically shown in list.

presidents' agendas. In short, even though these three officers ordinarily occupy similar positions on an institution's organizational chart, and even though the title conferred on the chief student affairs officer (for example, vice-president for student affairs) often suggests a status equal to that of the chief fiscal and academic officers, these data suggest that the chief student affairs officer's actual status is somewhat lower. A study of salaries also supports this conclusion; chief student affairs officers are typically paid less than chief fiscal or academic officers (Astin, 1977a).

Presidents communicate personally with students about as frequently as they do with their chief student affairs officers. However, it is remarkable that three of the forty-four presidents report that they average less than one personal contact with students every month. The characteristics of their three institutions suggest no particular pattern: a small religious institution on the West Coast, a women's college in the East, and a large commuter institution in the Midwest.

Perhaps even more remarkable is that presidents, on the average, converse with visitors about as often as they do with students. This finding raises an interesting question about the priorities of the typical college administrator: Is it reasonable to consider students and visitors as equally important? Is one hour's worth of conversation with a visitor of equal benefit to the institution as an hour's conversation with a student? While most presidents would probably not be willing to admit that they regard visitors as equal in importance to students, these data suggest that, in allocating their time, many presidents implicitly assign equal priority to these two groups. It might be a useful exercise for institutional chief executives to scrutinize their appointment calendars carefully to determine if their stated priorities coincide with their actual schedules.

Next in order are the two general groups of other academic administrators (provosts, deans, and assistant and associate deans) and other administrators (vice-presidents for administration, directors of development, and directors of institutional research). While the typical president does not meet with such administrators on a daily basis, most presidents interact at least several times a week with both of these two categories of administrators.

Considering the problems that the presidents encounter in their interactions with faculty, it is hardly surprising to find faculty so far down on the list of persons with whom presidents interact personally. Apparently, such interaction takes place about as often as interaction with potential donors. Indeed, *no* president fails to interact with potential donors at least once a month, whereas three presidents fail to interact with faculty as frequently as once a month. Again, these three presidents came from quite different types of institutions: a small college in the Midwest, a medium sized college in the South, and a somewhat larger urban college in the Northeast.

Presidential contact with the next group listed in Table 6, potential students, is highly varied: A substantial minority of presidents (nineteen of the forty-four who responded to this item) see potential students less than once a month. Twenty of the remaining twenty-five see them once a month or several times a month. Of the remaining five, three see potential students several times a week, while the other two report seeing potential students about *once a day*. Of particular interest here is that the enrollments of these last two institutions—both small liberal arts colleges—have grown substantially during recent years. This suggests that small private liberal arts colleges may be able to greatly increase their attractiveness to potential students if the chief executives become directly involved in the recruiting process.

The relatively low frequency of presidential interaction with middle managers confirms the generally low status of these institutional administrators, particularly the registrars and financial aid officers. The admissions officer seems to have somewhat more frequent interaction than the other two, possibly because of the direct connection between an institution's financial health and its enrollment. Note that every president interacts personally with his or her admissions officer at least once a month, and two presidents report interacting on a daily basis. In contrast, at five institutions the president fails to interact even once a month with either the financial aid officer or the registrar, indicating that these officers generally carry out policies made by others while the admissions officers participate in decision making.

Can the frequency of personal contact with the president be regarded as an index of an administrator's status within the institution? Recent data on the average annual salary paid to various administrators ("Administrators' Salaries . . . ," 1979) reveal a near-perfect correspondence between the median salaries paid to various categories of institutional administrators and their frequency of personal contact with the president: chief academic officer, $27,500; chief fiscal officer, $24,378; chief student affairs officer, $22,750; admissions officer, $18,500; financial aid officer, $15,547; and registrar, $17,568. Except for the reversal involving the last two administrators (financial aid officer and registrar), the rankings in median salary and in frequency of personal communication with the president are identical.

Another set of items on the presidential questionnaire concern the *means* by which the president communicates: staff or other intermediaries, letters or memoranda, personal telephone calls, personal conversations, formal group meetings, and informal meetings. Presidents were asked whether they used each of these means "frequently," "occasionally," or "seldom or never" to communicate with their staffs, other administrators, faculty, and students. Table 7 shows the proportion of the forty-four presidents who use each means frequently to communicate with each of these groups. The president's inner circle of top administrators (the chief academic and fiscal officers) is once again distinguished by having the most frequent personal contact: Three fourths of the presidents report communicating with these two officers frequently by telephone, and all forty-four presidents report having frequent personal conversations with them. These two administrators, as well as the chief student affairs officer, also have frequent formal and informal meetings with the president. The president's pattern of communication with the chief student affairs officer is very similar to that for the chief academic and fiscal officers, with one exception: The president is much less likely to talk with the chief student affairs officer on the telephone. This finding suggests that the most sensitive index of a person's status within an academic institution may be the frequency with which the president telephones that person.

Although few presidents communicate frequently by any means with either faculty or students, most of the presidents have occasional personal conversations and formal and informal meetings with these groups. Only one president seldom or never has formal meetings with faculty, and only four seldom have informal meetings. The pattern for meetings with students is the reverse: Four presidents seldom have formal meetings, and only one seldom meets informally with students. Somewhat surprisingly, substantial numbers of presidents seldom or never meet with department chairpersons either formally (eight) or informally (thirteen), although the majority of these colleges are relatively small.

**Table 7. Modes of Presidential Communication with Various Members of the Academic Community (N = 44 presidents)**

| | Percentage of Presidents Who Frequently Communicate by Means of | | | | | |
|---|---|---|---|---|---|---|
| Person(s) Communicated With | Staff or Other Intermediaries | Letters or Memoranda | Telephone Calls | Personal Conversations | Formal Group Meetings | Informal Meetings |
| Immediate staff | 14 | 14 | 27 | 100 | 30 | 82 |
| Chief academic officer | 16 | 16 | 73 | 100 | 71 | 77 |
| Chief fiscal officer | 16 | 16 | 77 | 100 | 73 | 80 |
| Chief student affairs officer | 18 | 18 | 30 | 86 | 71 | 68 |
| Admissions officer | 7 | 7 | 21 | 32 | 5 | 16 |
| Department chairs (collectively) | 14 | 5 | 2 | 9 | 0 | 0 |
| Other faculty | 21 | 11 | 16 | 23 | 7 | 7 |
| Students | 14 | 11 | 9 | 27 | 11 | 23 |

## How Others See the President

Items concerning frequency of communication with others were also included on the questionnaires of six other administrators: chief academic officer, chief fiscal officer, chief student affairs officer, admissions officer, financial aid officer, and registrar. Do the perceptions of these administrators as to their frequency of communication with the president agree with the president's own perceptions? To explore this question, the responses of these other administrators to the item concerning frequency of communication with the president were correlated with the president's own responses. Results are shown in Table 8. A comparison of the means shows considerable agreement, with the chief academic and fiscal officers having the highest means and the financial aid officer and registrar having the lowest means. With the exception of a reversal involving the registrar and the financial aid officer, the rank ordering of the two sets of means is identical. It should be noted, however, that the president is inclined to report somewhat greater frequency of communication than the person being communicated

Table 8. **Agreement on Frequency of Personal Contacts with the Presidents ($N$ = 33 institutions)**

| Person Communicated With | Mean[a] Frequency of Personal Contact as Reported by | | Correlation Between the Two Reports |
|---|---|---|---|
| | President | Person Communicated With | |
| Chief academic officer | 5.00 | 4.88 | .25 |
| Chief fiscal officer | 4.58 | 4.10 | .50 |
| Chief student affairs officer | 4.19 | 3.94 | .48 |
| Admissions officer | 3.16 | 3.06 | .58 |
| Financial aid officer | 2.23 | 1.97 | .05 |
| Registrar | 2.16 | 3.06 | .36 |

[a] Frequencies are expressed numerically according to the following scale: 6 = several times a day; 5 = about once a day; 4 = several times each week; 3 = about once a week; 2 = monthly; and 1 = less than monthly.

with. The one exception to this rule is the registrar, who reports substantially greater communication with the president (about once a week) than the president does with him or her (about once a month).

The last column of Table 8 shows the correlations between the two reports on frequency of communication. Although five of the six correlations were statistically significant ($p < .05$), there is wide variability in the magnitude of the coefficients. The relatively low agreement between the reports of the president and of the chief academic officer ($r = .25$) may result from the restricted variability on this item: All of the discrepancies in individual reports involved differences of only one category (that is, between "several times a day" and "about once a day," or between "once a day" and "several times each week"). Reports of the chief fiscal officer, the chief student affairs officer, and the admissions officer agree fairly closely, although an item such as this is subject to a considerable degree of interpretation by the respondent. Why agreement between the financial aid officer and the president should be so low is difficult to explain. Beyond the fact that this question, like the one for the chief academic officer, shows restricted variability in response, it may well be that the nature of the typical communication between the president and the financial aid officer leads to some discrepancy in interpreting just what a *personal* contact is. Whatever the explanation, these results suggest that reports of individual presidents and of financial aid officers about their frequency of personal contact must be viewed with considerable caution.

Faculty and administrator perceptions of the college president's style of operation were assessed in the questionnaire by means of an open-ended question: "How would you characterize your college president's style of operation?" The responses to this question fall into eight categories: open, efficient, remote, democratic, authoritarian, entrepreneurial, ineffective, and intellectual. (See Appendix E for more information about the coding scheme.)

To obtain a score for each president on each of the eight traits, the percentage of faculty and administrators whose responses could be coded into a given trait category was calculated. Table 9 shows the distribution of these scores for the twenty-eight

**Table 9. Ratings of Presidential Style by Faculty and Administrators: Distributions of Institutional Scores (N = 28 institutions)**

| Presidential Trait | Mean Institutional Score[a] | Distribution of Institutional Scores (Percentages)[a] | | | | | | | | | |
|---|---|---|---|---|---|---|---|---|---|---|---|
| | | 0–9 | 10–19 | 20–29 | 30–39 | 40–49 | 50–59 | 60–69 | 70–79 | 80–89 | 90–100 |
| Open | 39 | | 4 | 4 | 7 | 6 | 5 | 2 | | | |
| Efficient | 38 | | 5 | 4 | 4 | 10 | 3 | 1 | | 1 | |
| Remote | 22 | 4 | 12 | 5 | 4 | 2 | 1 | | | | |
| Authoritarian | 18 | 8 | 10 | 8 | | 1 | 1 | | | | |
| Democratic | 16 | 10 | 11 | 4 | 2 | | 1 | | | | |
| Entrepreneurial | 12 | 16 | 6 | 4 | 2 | | | | | | |
| Ineffective | 9 | 23 | 2 | 2 | | 1 | | | | | |
| Intellectual | 9 | 21 | 4 | 2 | 1 | | | | | | |

[a]Percentage of faculty and administrators who spontaneously mention the trait in response to the open-ended question, "How would you characterize your college president's style of operation?"

institutions at which at least ten faculty members responded to this question. Presidents are most likely to be described in terms of two positive traits: open and efficient. These two trait scores show similar distributions across the twenty-eight institutions, with scores ranging from less than 20 percent of the raters to more than 60 percent. The next two most frequently cited traits, however, involve negative characteristics: remoteness and authoritarianism. Once again the range of institutional scores on these traits is considerable, from less than 10 percent of the faculty and administrators to more than 50 percent. The last four traits—two positive and two negative—produce highly skewed distributions of scores, with the majority of institutional presidents scoring below 20 percent.

*Summary.* While these descriptive data from questionnaire and interview responses are intended primarily to introduce the variables used in later analyses and to generalize about this group of college presidents, some surprising findings emerge, even at this level. First, in spite of almost universal agreement that higher education has reached or is quickly approaching a "steady state," these presidents are overwhelmingly optimistic about the future of their institutions' financial state and enrollment. It is impossible to know or to evaluate the reasons for their optimism; indeed, such an attitude may be simply unrealistic and naive. Second, the repeated mention of difficulty with the faculty is disturbing. Reinforcing this impression is a statement by a college president, quoted by Kauffman (1978) in a recent article: "Perhaps the most difficult problem for the president is the realization that if he does his job well under contemporary conditions, he almost certainly will be disliked by faculty. Indeed, a trustee once said to me that if the faculty praised my performance, he would be suspicious that I was not carrying out the wishes of the board or pursuing the well-being of the institution as a whole. I suspect that in all but the most well-endowed institutions today, faculty desires are at cross-purposes with institutional well-being and the president is fated to be at cross-purposes with the professional group from which he is drawn" (p. 62).

Is this hostility a natural state, or is it attributable to some current condition, perhaps impending unionism? And what accounts for the ambivalence of the presidents toward the faculty: Why do they praise the faculty as classroom instructors but criticize them in practically every other role? While the data provide no answer to this question, the discussion of faculty outcomes in Chapter Five treats the relationships between presidential style, administrative type, and faculty satisfaction.

## The Other Administrators

While the president is obviously included under the umbrella heading of administrators, in this section, for simplicity, the term refers to the vice-presidential officers and some of the middle-level administrators. Questionnaires were completed by the following groups: vice-presidential officers (45 academic officers, 32 fiscal officers, 32 development officers, and 39 student affairs officers) and middle-level administrators (42 registrars, 40 admissions officers, and 36 financial aid officers).

In the sections that follow, we first present some summary information on the group of administrators as a whole: their general characteristics, their perceptions of their institutions' strengths and weaknesses, their predictions for the future, and the formal and informal organizational patterns that prevail among them. We then look at each type of administrator, drawing on interview data as well as questionnaire data. (Appendix F contains a detailed account of these data for each group of nonpresidential administrators.)

The reader should note that the measures below are *mean* scores computed separately for each institution. These means are based on the responses of all administrators (except the president), a group which typically includes the chief academic officer, the chief fiscal officer, the chief student affairs officer, the registrar, the director of admissions, and the director of student financial aid. Some institutions also have a chief planning officer who is included in all the analyses. Since only a few of the larger institutions have deans of various schools, they are not included in the questionnaire analyses, although their responses to the personal interviews are considered. The number of administrators whose responses were used to compute these scores varies between four and eight, with a mean of six. Complete data on each administrative variable were obtained for forty-one institutions.

*Descriptive Profile.* The average age of all the administrators in the sample is forty-five years. Fiscal officers are the oldest group, averaging forty-nine years of age, and admissions officers are the youngest, averaging thirty-nine years.

Overall, about four in five of the administrators are men, though the sex distribution varies by position. Thus, 88 percent of the vice-presidential officers are male, and there are no female fiscal officers. Of the middle-level administrators, 68 percent are men and 32 percent are women, a distribution that is consistent with earlier findings (Astin, 1977a).

The educational attainment of the administrators also varies by position. While 91 percent of the academic vice-presidents have the doctoral degree, only 19 percent of the other vice-presidential administrators and only 8 percent of the middle managers hold the doctorate.

These administrators have been at their institutions for an average of ten years, except for registrars, who average fifteen years. Since the standard deviation in all cases is roughly nine years, however, the only conclusion that can be drawn is that the length of time an administrator spends at an institution varies greatly.

Almost a third of these administrators have taught under-graduates within the three years prior to the survey. While this is most likely to be true of the academic and student affairs officers, a larger-than-expected proportion of other administrators are former faculty members.

*Perceived Strengths and Weaknesses of the Institution.* The two top-ranked institutional strengths as perceived by these administra-tors are institutional reputation and the quality of teaching; most groups mention the former most frequently, but the academic officers and the registrars resemble the president in more often mentioning the latter. The third-ranked strength differs according to the position of the respondent: for both academic officers and admissions officers, it is the scope of curricular offerings; for fiscal officers and financial aid officers, it is financial soundness. Student affairs officers concur with the presidents in rating impact on students' academic development as the third strength; impact on students' personal development is cited by development officers; and academic freedom is mentioned by registrars.

The most frequently mentioned institutional weakness, among all but the financial aid officers, is financial soundness. Development officers mention alumni support just as often, financial aid officers cite it most often, and the academic and fiscal officers rank it second, as do the presidents. Faculty morale is ranked second as an institutional quality in need of improvement by three groups: student affairs officers, registrars, and admissions officers; it is ranked third by development and financial aid officers. Like the presidents, fiscal officers, student affairs officers, admissions officers, and financial aid officers are also inclined to believe that the institution's impact on students' personal or character development should be strengthened. Finally, institutional reputation ranks third as a weakness among academic officers; the curious point here is that this same characteristic is often cited as a strength.

*Predictions of Change.* These administrators are generally even more optimistic about prospects for increased institutional revenues than the presidents are (see Table 5). Overall, 84 percent predict increases in budgets. Differing from the presidents, however, 52 percent of these administrators predict no change in the numbers of new faculty, and only 28 percent predict decreases. They are also inclined to differ from the presidents with respect to number of tenured faculty: 52 percent foresee no change, and 33 percent foresee increases.

Administrators are slightly more optimistic than are presidents about future growth in the applicant pool and in enrollment: 38 percent predict growth in the latter. Only 11 percent predict decreases in the numbers of either applicants or enrollments.

Unlike the presidents, a majority of administrators (54 percent) anticipate increasing board involvement in the college's operations. Administrators generally see little or no change in total faculty size, in student quality, in the number of majors offered, in externally funded research, and in noneducational enterprises sponsored by the college. In all of these "steady state" areas, they concur with the president.

The obvious generalization is that administrators are more optimistic about the future than might be expected. To an even greater extent than the presidents, these administrators present a picture of a group of educators seemingly confident that their colleges can overcome existing financial pressures and competition for students. Both their judgments about the strong points of their institutions and their predictions for the future reinforce this image.

*Formal and Informal Organizational Patterns.* An examination of the organization chart (Figure 1) from the colleges in the sample reveals that all of the institutions have an academic officer and a fiscal officer who report directly to the president. In most colleges, the student affairs officer also reports directly to the president, although in a few cases, he or she reports directly to the academic officer. Further, many colleges have a director of development who is at the same level or who reports either to the fiscal officer or to the academic officer. While the title of these officials varies from vice-president to director or dean, these four positions are clearly vice-presidential posts at most colleges.

As for middle-level administrators, financial aid officers usually report to the student affairs vice-president but are sometimes directly under the authority of the academic or fiscal vice-president and in one case reports directly to the president. Registrars most often report to the academic vice-president; in the only two exceptions, they report to the student affairs director. The admissions officer also reports to the academic vice-president in most institutions, although there is more variation in this position than in any other. The admissions officers report directly to the president in three colleges, to the development officer in two others, and to other vice-presidents in still other institutions. Given the exceptions as noted, the organizational structure for the administrators included in the sample is that pictured in Figure 1.

**Figure 1. Typical College Organization Chart**

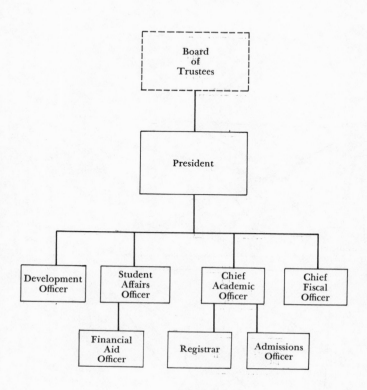

Clues to the informal structure of the administration come from reports of personal interactions both among administrators and between administrators and others in the college community (see Tables 7 and 10). Figure 2 shows patterns of frequent communication and illustrates the normal bureaucratic structure of these institutions as well as presenting some anomalies. The average president is fairly isolated in that his most frequent two-way communication is with his inner circle of staff and vice-presidents, with somewhat less communication with the student affairs officer than with the others. The exception to this isolation is his contact

## Figure 2. Administrative Sociogram

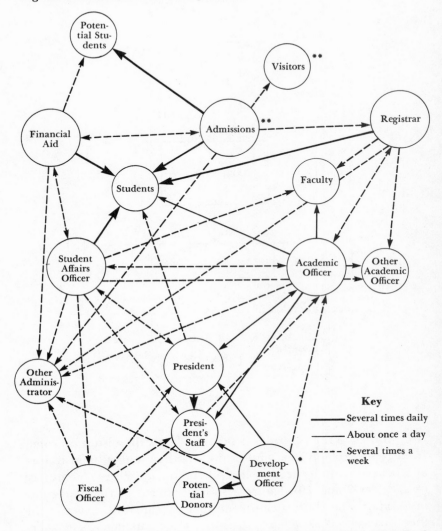

*The development officer responded to the questionnaire but the position was not listed. Other large circles represent officers who responded and whose positions were listed.

**Small circles represent positions listed, but persons occupying the positions did not respond to a questionnaire.

Table 10. Frequency of Personal Contact Between Administrators and Other Members of the Campus Community

| Person or Group Contacted by Administrators[a] | Mean of Institutional Means[b] | Range of Institutional Means | |
|---|---|---|---|
| | | Lowest | Highest |
| Students | 4.95 | 3.86 | 5.71 |
| Staff of chief executive officer | 4.09 | 3.29 | 5.14 |
| Faculty (excluding chairs) | 3.77 | 2.57 | 5.14 |
| Chief fiscal or planning officer | 3.74 | 2.50 | 4.83 |
| Chief student affairs officer | 3.67 | 2.50 | 5.60 |
| Chief admissions officer | 3.62 | 2.17 | 4.83 |
| Chief academic officer | 3.55 | 2.67 | 4.67 |
| Chief executive officer | 3.38 | 2.29 | 4.29 |
| Registrar | 3.36 | 2.00 | 4.33 |
| Financial aid officer | 3.28 | 2.17 | 5.00 |

[a] All administrators other than the president (mean number of respondents at each institution is six).

[b] Frequencies are expressed numerically according to the following scale: 6 = several times daily; 5 = about once a day; 4 = several times each week; 3 = about once a week; 2 = monthly; and 1 = less than once a month.

with students. The other administrators also behave much as might be expected: They communicate with those on their own level, with their "clientele," and with their immediate superiors and subordinates. Admissions officers are something of an exception in that they appear to be isolated from their immediate superiors. The sociogram, however, is based on averages and, as previously noted, the admissions officers show the greatest variation in their positions on the organization chart; they also show less of a pattern in their reports on communication style than do their peers, the registrars and the financial aid officers. As mentioned before, in some colleges, admissions officers occupy a higher position than their title indicates.

It is also clear from Figure 2 that the academic officer is in a central position for both giving and receiving information and apparently serves as a channel through which the president and other vice-presidents reach the faculty. The reader should note that this sociogram depicts only the administrators considered in this study. If deans from the larger colleges and department chairs had been included, and if responses from faculty and students had been diagrammed as well, additional patterns would emerge.

*Sources of Information.* Each administrator's questionnaire contained a list of items preceded by the following question: "How often do you rely on the following sources to find out what goes on in other areas of the administration?" Each administrator was asked to respond to ten alternatives representing sources of information (Table 11) in the following response mode: frequently, occasionally, seldom or never.

Not surprisingly, most administrators in most of the institutions frequently get their information about other areas of the administration by talking directly with fellow administrators. Nevertheless, a good deal of information is also obtained through

**Table 11. Administrators' Sources of Information About Other Areas of the Administration (N = 41 institutions)**

| | Degree of Reliance[b] on Source | | |
| | | Range of Institutional Means | |
| Source of Administrators'[a] Information | Mean of Institutional Means | Lowest | Highest |
|---|---|---|---|
| Personal conversations with people involved | 2.86 | 2.29 | 3.00 |
| Meetings | 2.62 | 2.14 | 3.00 |
| Memoranda | 2.31 | 1.86 | 2.86 |
| Newsletters | 1.84 | 1.14 | 2.43 |
| Gossip, hearsay, or through the grapevine | 1.77 | 1.14 | 2.14 |
| Student newspaper | 1.67 | 1.14 | 2.43 |
| Through the faculty | 1.50 | 1.14 | 2.14 |
| Formal reports | 1.27 | 1.00 | 1.71 |

[a] All administrators except the president (mean number of respondents at each institution is six).

[b] Reliance is expressed numerically according to the following scale: 3 = frequently; 2 = occasionally; and 1 = seldom or never.

meetings and, to a lesser extent, memoranda. Newsletters are relied upon occasionally by the typical administrator, although in
some institutions, most administrators seldom or never get their
information from newsletters. The next three alternatives—the
faculty, the student newspaper, and "gossip, hearsay, or through
the grapevine"—might all be classified as indirect sources of administrative information. Administrators in different colleges vary
considerably in the extent to which they rely on such indirect
sources. The final information source, formal reports, is seldom or
never relied upon by most administrators.

*The Reward System.* One of the most revealing sets of items in
the administrators' questionnaires is their responses to the following question: "How do you value the following behaviors in your
professional subordinates?" Each administrator was asked to respond to each of seventeen traits according to the following
categories: very important, somewhat important, not important,
and negative characteristic. Administrators were also asked: "In
your judgment, on what basis are administrators rewarded at your
institution?" In this case, respondents indicated the extent to which
each of a similar list of traits was very descriptive, somewhat descriptive, or not descriptive of behavior leading to reward. These
two lists can be regarded as a kind of projective test revealing
whether administrators think that their colleagues value the same
traits as they themselves do.

Results of both of these analyses are given in Table 12. Since
the mode of response was different for the two lists, the ranking of
each item on each list is shown to facilitate comparison.

The same four traits—cooperation, initiative, interpersonal
skills, and professional or technical competence—occupy the top
four ranks in both lists. In short, not only do most administrators in
most institutions consider these four traits to be very important in
their subordinates, but also they feel that administrators are rewarded for displaying these traits. It is interesting that professional
or technical competence seems to be slightly less important than the
other three traits. The variation in institutional means on these
four traits is extremely limited—from 3.8 to 3.9 on the "subordinates" list and from 2.6 to 2.8 on the "reward" list.

**Table 12. Relative Importance of Various Traits as Perceived by Administrators (N = 41 institutions)**

| Trait | How Much Administrators Value Trait in Subordinates | | How Much Administrators Say Trait Describes Behavior That Is Rewarded | | Rank Differ- |
| --- | --- | --- | --- | --- | --- |
| | Mean[a] | Rank | Mean[b] | Rank | ence |
| Cooperation | 3.94 | 1–2 | 2.78 | 1–2 | 0 |
| Initiative | 3.94 | 1–2 | 2.72 | 3 | −1 |
| Interpersonal skills | 3.87 | 3 | 2.63 | 4 | −1 |
| Professional or technical competence | 3.82 | 4 | 2.78 | 1–2 | +2 |
| Frankness in dealing with others | 3.79 | 5 | 2.28 | 8 | −3 |
| Effectiveness in dealing with students | 3.78 | 6 | 2.51 | 6 | 0 |
| Creativity | 3.68 | 7 | 2.48 | 7 | 0 |
| Willingness to accept authority | 3.52 | 8 | 2.57 | 5 | +3 |
| Support from faculty | 3.45 | 9 | 2.20 | 9 | 0 |
| Aggressiveness | 3.14 | 10 | 2.17 | 10 | 0 |
| Personal ambition | 3.05 | 11 | 2.00 | 11–12 | 0 |
| Scholarship | 3.02 | 12 | 1.98 | 13 | −1 |
| Willingness to take risks | 3.00 | 13–14 | 2.00 | 11–12 | +2 |
| Salesmanship | 3.00 | 13–14 | 1.94 | 14 | 0 |
| Competitiveness | 2.53 | 15 | 1.88 | 16 | −1 |
| Influence with those in power | 2.51 | 16 | 1.91 | 15 | +1 |
| Willingness to apple-polish | 1.27 | 17 | 1.22 | 17 | 0 |
| Nepotism or "buddyism" | — | — | 1.29 | — | — |

[a] Administrators' responses are expressed numerically according to the following scale: 4 = very important; 3 = somewhat important; 2 = not important; and 1 = negative.
[b] Administrators' responses are expressed numerically according to the following scale: 3 = very descriptive; 2 = somewhat descriptive; and 1 = not descriptive.

Generally speaking, the ranking of the different traits is similar in both lists. Eight of the seventeen items have identical ranks, another five differ by only one rank, and only two items differ by as much as three ranks. Administrators are inclined to think that they value frankness more highly than their administrative colleagues do but that their colleagues place more value on willingness to accept authority, willingness to take risks, and—somewhat surprisingly—professional or technical competence.

While the means rankings of the items in Table 12 represent the average of the responses, the means for some of the items vary substantially from one institution to the other. The greatest degree of variability in the "subordinates" list is associated with the traits of scholarship (from 2.43 to 3.71), aggressiveness (from 2.49 to 3.87), competitiveness (from 1.71 to 3.14), and influence with those in power (from 2.00 to 3.29). Three of these same items also show considerable variability from institution to institution in the "reward" list: aggressiveness (from 1.71 to 2.71), influence with those in power (from 1.29 to 2.43), and competitiveness (from 1.43 to 2.43). Other items in this list which show considerable variability are willingness to apple-polish (from 1.00 to 2.14), salesmanship (from 1.29 to 2.43), effectiveness in dealing with students (from 1.86 to 3.00), and nepotism or "buddyism" (from 1.00 to 2.00).

In sum, these findings suggest that traits such as cooperation, initiative, interpersonal skills, and professional or technical competence are almost universally valued by administrators. Traits such as aggressiveness and competitiveness, in contrast, are valued and rewarded at some institutions but not at others. Finally, even though negative traits such as willingness to apple-polish and nepotism or "buddyism" are regarded unfavorably by virtually all administrators in most institutions, a few institutions seem to reward the display of such traits.

## Summary

The general tone of the responses of college administrators (which are described in detail in Appendix F) is positive. Most believe that their institution has a good overall reputation and that the quality of the teaching is high. They are highly optimistic about the future of their institutions, being especially likely to anticipate increases in funding from various sources. Their values, as reflected in their reports of the traits they want subordinates to have, put them clearly on the side of the angels: Initiative, cooperation, interpersonal skills, and professional or technical competence are rated high by most groups of administrators, and relatively few mention such traits as willingness to apple-polish, influence with those in power, and personal ambition. The majority are satisfied with such intrinsic features of their jobs as challenge, responsibility, and variety in activities.

Nonetheless, paradise has some serpents. For instance, administrators are likely to feel that their institutions are somewhat weak with respect to financial soundness, alumni support, and faculty morale. Moreover, the different groups of administrators experience dissatisfaction with some aspects of their jobs and face various frustrations and problems, which vary depending on their position. Generally speaking, the higher the position, the greater the job satisfaction. The following paragraphs summarize the outstanding characteristics of each group of administrators covered in this study.

College presidents tend to be the most satisfied group of administrators, finding both the intrinsic and the extrinsic features of their jobs rewarding. Nonetheless, the very importance of their position exacts a toll; they are less likely than other administrators to express satisfaction with their opportunities for scholarly pursuits, for time with their families, and for leisure activities. Moreover, only about two in five are very satisfied with the status of their institution, although many cite institutional reputation as a strength. Even more contradictory is their attitude toward faculty: Although they praise the faculty's teaching and apparently value their opinions, they also say that the faculty often inhibits or frustrates them.

The same ambivalent attitude is apparent among the chief academic officers, who are even more likely than the presidents to have come from scholarly or academic backgrounds. They have a strong faculty orientation—naming faculty as the associates whose opinions they value most and turning to them for advice—but they also say that the faculty's arrogance, conservatism, and naivete cause them frustration. Moreover, their toughest decisions involve the hiring, promotion, tenure, and firing of faculty members. (Similarly, the vice-presidential officers, with the exception of student affairs officers, seem to agonize most over personnel decisions.) Academic officers are also somewhat more skeptical than others about the reputation of the institution, citing it as in need of strengthening and expressing dissatisfaction with the status of their institutions.

Though fiscal officers encounter no such problems with faculty, having relatively few dealings with them, they manifest some discontent with their opportunities for advancement within their own institutions and the unlikelihood of their being offered jobs at other institutions. In some sense, they feel themselves to be in dead-end positions, because they lack the credentials and academic background necessary to rise to college presidencies. In the interviews, many state that if they could do things differently, they would have taken more formal training. To some extent, fiscal officers seem remote from the daily life of the campus. They tend to be dissatisfied with the congeniality of their work relationships, and they often turn for advice to people who have nó connection with the college: personal friends, the business officers of other institutions, bankers, and outside consultants. Their toughest decisions involve the firing of personnel (especially those who might have a hard time finding other jobs), financial issues (for example, how to invest money), and student financial problems (for example, whether students should be dismissed for not paying their bills).

Development officers are also likely to be somewhat isolated from campus life and to seek advice from people who have no connection with the college: the development officers of other institutions and outside consultants. They have less contact with students than does any other group but are much more likely to frequently see potential donors. Their orientation is toward business rather than toward academe, as is reflected in their inclination to say that the general process of academic governance is their greatest source of frustration. In some ways, development officers seem to be the most entrepreneurial group of administrators. Three in ten report earning outside incomes of more than $5,000 a year, and they are much more likely than others to say that they value in their subordinates such traits as salesmanship, aggressiveness, personal ambition, and competitiveness. Like other vice-presidential officers, however, they find personnel decisions the toughest to resolve, followed by general administrative problems and financial matters. Finally, they tend to be more dissatisfied than other vice-presidential officers with their salary, status, power, and employment opportunities both within their own institutions and at other institutions; perhaps their dissatisfaction on these points stems from a tendency to compare themselves with their peers in the business world rather than with their colleagues in academe.

Though student affairs officers are shown on formal organization charts as having equal status with other vice-presidential officers, they seem to have somewhat lower status than the others, perhaps because students (a low-status group) constitute their chief clientele. Though generally dissatisfied with their status, power, and influence, they are more likely than most other groups of administrators to say they are very satisfied with their relations with students and the congeniality of their coworkers. Their toughest decisions involve disciplining students, although like the other vice-presidents they also find personnel decisions difficult. Interestingly, not one mentions students as being a source of frustration; rather, they are likely to cite general administrative problems, the faculty, and lack of time. Moreover, they are more likely than other groups to say that they are frustrated by the basic conservatism of the institution. Though somewhat cut off from the power centers, student affairs officers have frequent contact with, and turn for advice to, faculty, students, deans, and clergy (the last a group not mentioned by other administrators).

Of the middle managers covered by this study, registrars are most likely to say that their greatest frustrations involve procedures (for example, data processing) rather than people. Like fiscal officers, but for different reasons, they seem to have dead-end jobs that offer few opportunities for upward mobility but are generally less demanding than other administrative jobs, leaving them more free time for scholarly pursuits, family life, and leisure activities. On the whole, they seem somewhat resigned to their positions, meeting frustration with a stoic attitude and accepting their relative lack of input into the administrative process as appropriate to their positions.

Admissions officers are the youngest group of administrators and are more satisfied—especially with their status and their visibility for jobs at other institutions—than are other middle managers. Their most frequent personal contacts are, understandably, with potential students and visitors, though they are also in closer touch with the top administrators than are registrars or financial aid officers. Aside from difficulties with other administrators and administrative offices and general administrative problems, their chief sources of frustration are lack of time and frequent interruptions. Most seem to feel that they have adequate input into administrative decision making, confirming the notion mentioned earlier that admissions officers have somewhat greater power and status than is indicated by formal organizational charts.

Financial aid officers are the most dissatisfied group of administrators covered in this study on all but two counts: They are more likely than others to give high ratings to their relations with students and to the competency of their colleagues. Like registrars, they are generally cut off from the administrative power centers; their most frequent contacts are with students and potential students. They name a variety of other campus offices as their chief source of frustration, and they are also more likely than are other administrators to complain of staff shortages. Asked whether they have adequate input into the administrative process, only one gave an unqualified affirmative response.

Several major questions arise from this brief descriptive summary of college administrators. The first has already been discussed but deserves to be repeated: Why is there such animosity between presidents and chief academic officers, on the one hand, and faculty, on the other? The attitudes of these administrators toward the faculty are, at best, ambivalent: They speak highly of the quality of teaching but they also accuse faculty of arrogance, mindless opposition to change, and an imperfect grasp of reality. To what extent are these charges justified? What can be said on the faculty's side? Can the tension be resolved, or is it an inevitable concomitant of academic life?

The second question, also touched on previously, concerns the administrators' views of the future of the institution. It would seem that their overwhelming optimism about several areas—especially funding and enrollment—is unwarranted in the light of current financial stringencies and population trends. Why are administrators so hopeful about the future? Are they not being unrealistic, refusing to accept the idea that bad things could happen to their institutions?

The final question—and one that has serious implications for education—involves the relatively low status of those administrators who deal most frequently and most closely with students: the student affairs officer and the middle managers, especially the financial aid officer. Why do these positions carry so much less prestige than do, for instance, the positions of chief fiscal officer and development officer? The majority of institutions studied were private liberal arts colleges, most of them small—the very type of institution that is generally regarded as having a deep commitment to student development. It seems a sad commentary on the values of college administrators that, even in these colleges, the officers who are most directly concerned with student welfare should be accorded so little honor.

# THREE

# *Four Presidential Styles*

In Chapter Two we presented a portrait of the "typical" private college president. This chapter examines a number of questions concerning *differences* in various presidents' styles of institutional management. How do these presidents differ in the ways they approach their jobs? Are there identifiable management styles? How closely do the presidents' views of their own styles of operation correspond to the perceptions of their administrative colleagues, faculty, and students? Are certain presidential styles more likely to be found in certain types of institutions?

The data used to explore these questions come from several sources: the presidents' descriptions of their own administrative behavior as reflected in their questionnaire responses; the presidents' self-characterizations as revealed in personal interviews; other administrators' descriptions of presidential behavior and style as indicated in questionnaires and personal interviews; and faculty perceptions of presidential style.

## A Typology of Presidential Styles

Our attempts to identify unique presidential styles involve a series of factor analyses using thirty measures derived from three sources: the president's self-reported frequency of personal conversations with others (sixteen measures; see Table 6), faculty and administrator ratings of presidential style (eight measures; see Table 9), and the president's preferred mode of communication (six measures; see Table 7). These last six measures were obtained by averaging the president's responses (3 = frequently; 2 = occasionally; 1 = seldom or never) across the eight categories of persons communicated with. Three additional measures are also used: the percentage of time that the president reports spending on campus, the number of years that the president has been at the institution, and the president's age.

One simplistic way to use these data to identify different presidential styles would be to assume that each measure reflects a different style. Such an approach, however, ignores the substantial redundancy that normally occurs when this many measurements are taken on the same set of individuals. Accordingly, we submitted the thirty-three measures to a factor analysis to convert them into a much smaller number of more general style measures and minimize redundancy among the different measures.

Factor analysis accomplishes these aims by analyzing the patterns of correlations among the original variables. In effect, factor analysis permits us to express information on presidential styles contained in the original thirty-three measures in terms of a smaller number of hypothetical style factors. The meaning of each factor, in turn, is best understood by examining those variables with the highest factor loadings (a factor loading is the correlation between the factor and one of the original variables).

The factor analysis yields four different presidential style factors. (The thirty-three measures were intercorrelated and factor analyzed by the principal components method. Several different analytical and rotational schemes were attempted, but the most interpretable results were obtained from the first four—unrotated— principal components. Nevertheless, because of the very small sample size, the results should be interpreted with some caution.) An inspection of the highest loading variables prompts us to label these four presidential types as: the bureaucrat, the intellectual, the egalitarian, and the counselor. Each of these presidential types is discussed below.

*The Bureaucrat.* The bureaucrat is characterized by the following pattern of attributes:

|  | *Factor Loading* |
|---|---|
| *Persons frequently communicated with:* | |
| chief academic officer | .68 |
| chief fiscal officer | .63 |
| staff | .53 |
| chief student affairs officer | .49 |
| *Preferred mode of communication:* | |
| through staff or other intermediaries | .58 |
| *How perceived by faculty and administrators:* | |
| remote | .71 |
| ineffective | .71 |
| *not* open | −.69 |
| *not* efficient | −.57 |

The bureaucrat is more likely than are other presidential types to communicate frequently with top administrators (the chief fiscal and academic officers, in particular) and with immediate staff. Further, the bureaucrat tends to communicate indirectly through staff or other intermediaries rather than directly with the people involved. Not surprisingly, faculty and fellow administrators see the bureaucrat as remote and as not being open. The negative rating on efficiency suggests that faculty and administrative colleagues may regard the use of intermediaries as an inefficient mode of communication. The reason that the bureaucrat is also seen as ineffective is less clear, although it may well be that a "halo effect" is operating here: Others may be inclined to see all aspects of the bureaucrat's functioning in a negative light.

*The Intellectual.* The intellectual has a very different pattern of characteristics:

|                                                    | Factor Loading |
| -------------------------------------------------- | -------------- |
| *Persons frequently communicated with:*            |                |
| faculty                                            | .79            |
| other administrators                               | .51            |
| other academic administrators                      | .45            |
| *not* registrar                                    | −.53           |
| *not* potential donors                             | −.40           |
| *How perceived by faculty and administrators:*     |                |
| intellectual                                       | .62            |

The most distinctive feature of the intellectual is frequent communication with faculty. (Though tempted to label this type the *faculty's man,* we hesitated to do so because of the sexist overtone of this designation.) That faculty should tend to regard such presidents as intellectual is hardly surprising, although it raises some interesting interpretative issues. Does the president's interacting frequently with faculty members make them feel that "he is one of our kind"? Or do the more intellectually oriented presidents interact frequently simply because they identify with the faculty?

The intellectual is also more likely to communicate with a group of other academic administrators that includes persons such as provosts, deans, and assistant deans who would ordinarily be closer to faculty, particularly in the more complex institutions. Why presidents of this type should communicate infrequently with the registrar is not immediately apparent, but their infrequent communication with potential donors raises interesting speculative possibilities: Could it be that they minimize the importance of such

presidential tasks as fund raising because they see their primary
loyalties and responsibilities as involving the faculty?

*The Egalitarian.* The egalitarian president is characterized
by still another pattern of items:

|  | Factor Loading |
|---|---|
| *Persons frequently communicated with:* | |
| students | .66 |
| registrar | .63 |
| financial aid officer | .62 |
| potential donors | .62 |
| potential students | .59 |
| visitors | .59 |
| faculty | .49 |
| *How perceived by faculty and administrators:* | |
| *not* authoritarian | −.43 |

The egalitarian communicates more often than do other
presidential types not just with faculty and students but with a wide
range of other people who are seen only infrequently by most college presidents: the registrar, the financial aid officer, potential donors, potential students, and visitors. This frenetic lifestyle suggests
that egalitarians find it difficult to establish any priorities in their
interpersonal contacts and hence devote small amounts of time
to each group within their wide range of constituents. Given their
apparent accessibility to almost any individual or group, it is hardly
surprising that egalitarians are seen as nonauthoritarian.

*The Counselor.* The fourth presidential type, the counselor,
is characterized by the following pattern of attributes:

|  | Factor Loading |
|---|---|
| *Preferred modes of communication:* | |
| personal conversations | .82 |
| informal meetings | .68 |

*Factor Loading*

*Persons frequently communicated with:*
 *not* consultants                                      −.44

*Demographic characteristics:*
 years at institution                                  .58
 age                                                   .44

*How perceived by faculty and administrators:*
 entrepreneurial                                       .43

The most distinctive feature of the counselor's administrative style is a preference for dealing with others by means of personal conversations and informal meetings. Counselors are likely to be older and to have been in office longer than the three other presidential types. One gets the impression here of a rather comfortable parental figure who conducts business in a personal and informal style. It is not surprising that such a person does not feel the need for help from outside consultants and is perceived as a good entrepreneur or fund raiser. It must be pointed out, however, that his being perceived as a good fund raiser may simply reflect the length of time the president has been at the institution: Good fund raisers are probably more likely to survive in their jobs than are presidents who are inept at that all-important task.

### Correlates of Presidential Style

Perhaps the best way to gain a fuller understanding of the four presidential types identified in the previous section is to determine if the presence or absence of a given type is associated with other attributes of the institution. For this purpose we first computed for each president a "score" corresponding to each of the four types. These scores consist of a weighted combination* of the

---

*Each high-loading item was first converted into a standard score (mean = 0; standard deviation = 1), and then weighted and summed arithmetically to obtain the factor score. Items with negative loadings were weighted by −1. All other items were given weights of +1, except for a few

highest-loading items listed under each presidential type (see the preceding section). In effect, these scores indicate how closely any actual president resembles each of the four hypothetical types. A president would receive a high score on the intellectual scale, for example, if he or she communicates frequently with faculty and other administrators, communicates infrequently with the registrar and with potential donors, and is perceived by the faculty as intellectual. Sufficient data were available to compute the four presidential style scores for each of thirty presidents.

A few presidents failed to obtain high scores on any of the types, whereas a few others obtained high scores on more than one type. For example, if we require that a president score at least one half of a standard deviation above the mean in order to be classified as belonging to any type, eleven presidents could not be classified. Of those that were single types, four were bureaucratic, three were intellectual, two each were egalitarian and counselors. Mixed style presidents included two intellectual-egalitarian, two egalitarian-counselor, and two bureaucratic-egalitarian. There was one intellectual-counselor and one intellectual-egalitarian-counselor.

These four presidential style scores were then correlated with data from four other sources: information on institutional characteristics, presidential interviews, interviews with other administrators, and measures of presidential job satisfaction. The results of these analyses are described below.

*Institutional Characteristics.* Each of the four presidential style scores was correlated with seventeen different measures of institutional characteristics: size (total enrollment); selectivity (mean total of Verbal and Mathematical SAT scores of entering freshmen; see Astin and Henson, 1977); affluence (per-student expenditures for educational and general expenditures); tuition; region (four dichotomous measures: East, South, Midwest, and West-Southwest);

---

of the highest-loading items which we gave weights of +2: communication with faculty for the intellectual type; personal conversations as a preferred conversation mode for the counselor type; and faculty observations of "remote" and "ineffective" for the bureaucratic type.

control (Protestant, Roman Catholic, nondenominational); sex (men only, women only, coeducational); race (predominantly black); and two measures of the local environment: urbanity (college's proximity to a population center of at least 500,000); and residential emphasis (ratio of students living in campus housing to total enrollment).

The bureaucratic president is significantly ($p < .05$) associated with four of the seventeen institutional characteristics. The bureaucrat is most likely to be found as president of large ($r = .50$) or nondenominational (.42) institutions and least likely to be found in Protestant colleges ($-.48$) or in colleges with a strong residential emphasis ($-.37$). That presidents of large colleges tend to operate in a more bureaucratic manner than presidents of small colleges no doubt reflects the more complex administrative structure that characterizes many larger institutions. Since the correlations with both Protestant and nondenominational control become nonsignificant when size is controlled by partial correlation techniques, it appears that Protestant colleges seldom have bureaucratic presidents primarily because they tend to be very small, and nondenominational colleges frequently have bureaucratic presidents because they tend to be larger than denominational colleges. The negative correlation with residential emphasis, which does not disappear when size is controlled, suggests that the impersonality of a commuter environment may be conducive to the development of a bureaucratic presidential style. Or, possibly, residential colleges recruit presidents who are not likely to operate in a bureaucratic way.

Presidents of the intellectual type are likely to be found at selective institutions (.35) and at institutions located in the East (.44). They are not likely to be found at midwestern institutions ($-.53$). These results are consistent with the stereotype of eastern institutions as emphasizing scholarship and intellectual concerns. Since intellectual presidents communicate frequently with faculty, these findings also confirm the notion that faculty in the more selective institutions tend to have more power and status than faculty in less selective institutions.

The geographical distribution of egalitarian presidents is the reverse of the pattern for intellectual presidents. They are frequently found in the Midwest (.34) and infrequently found in the East (−.41). To a certain extent, these results are consistent with the types of higher education systems found in these two regions: The Midwest has for many years operated many of its largest public universities on an open-admissions basis, while the East has traditionally emphasized academically elite institutions with selective admissions.

The fourth presidential type, the counselor, did not correlate significantly with any of the seventeen institutional characteristics.

*Presidential Interviews.* Do different types of presidents describe themselves differently in the personal interviews? While answers to this question must necessarily be tentative, given the relatively small number of presidents and the open-ended nature of the interviews, the richness of the material in many of these interviews warrants at least some attempt on our part to relate them to the four presidential styles.

First, we identified the three presidents with the highest scores and the three with the lowest scores in each of the four types. Next, the presidents' responses to the opening question from the personal interviews were coded in the categories discussed in Chapter Two (see Table 2). (The coder was not aware of how each president was classified.) Finally, the codes for the highest- and lowest-scoring presidents on each factor were compared. Any code that applied to all three presidents in one group (highs or lows) but to none in the other groups was considered as "discriminating."*

Perhaps the clearest discriminations occur with the presidents at the extremes on the intellectual factor. For example, in response to the question about major highlights and disappointments of the presidency, all three of the most intellectual presidents, and none of the least intellectual ones, mention problems with faculty as major disappointments: "I've not been able to effectively build a sense of trust in the faculty"; "The friction between

---

*Assuming an a priori probability of .5 that any code will be assigned to any president, the likelihood that all three in one group and none in the other will have a particular code is about .03.

faculty and students"; and "Faculty may think I do not feel as they do about academic matters." These same three presidents (and none of the three least intellectual presidents) also give responses reflecting academic concerns: "With good teaching we can hold our enrollment"; "We have spent too much time on fiscal rather than educational problems"; and "[More] planning in regard to basic curriculum, academic goals . . . evaluation of faculty."

These results are consistent with the notion that intellectual presidents are more concerned with academic affairs and with faculty than are other presidential types. It is of interest, however, that faculty are mentioned by all three intellectual presidents in the context of major *disappointments*. One could speculate that frequent presidential interaction with faculty carries with it certain risks, including disappointment and frustration at faculty obstructionism, conservatism, and hostility. Of course, it may also be that intellectual presidents' tendency to identify with the faculty leads them to have higher expectations for faculty than other presidential types have. When faculty fail to fulfill these expectations, the intellectual presidents may therefore be more prone to express their disappointments about faculty.

None of the three other presidential types had such clear-cut relationships with the open-ended interview responses. One other finding, nevertheless, deserves some brief discussion. Only two of the twenty-three presidents mention the campus unrest of the late 1960s and early 1970s as among their administrative highlights or disappointments. Not surprisingly, both of these presidents are counselor types. (The reader will recall that number of years at the institution is one of the variables used to define this type.) Both presidents view this period as one of their major highlights: "We came through the student uprising with no major blow-up"; and "[I saw] the students go through the period of intense blackness of the 1960s and emerge into an environment which takes into consideration their culture and history."

*Administrator Interviews.* The personal interviews conducted with key administrators on each campus include several questions relating directly to the president's administrative style and impact on the institution: "How would you characterize your president's style of operation?" We analyzed all the administrators' statements about the presidents to see if the high-scoring presidents on each style factor were perceived differently from their low-scoring counterparts. We identified eleven content categories: open or accessible, delegates responsibility well, good fund raiser, democratic, concerned with budgets, good at public relations, informal, concerned with academics, concerned with students, innovative, and concerned with faculty relations. A president is designated as possessing a given trait if between 25 and 50 percent (depending on the trait) of the interviewees spontaneously mentioned that trait in the interview. (If an interviewee mentioned an opposing or contradictory trait, the value minus one [−1] was added to the numerator before computing the percentage.) A trait is considered discriminating on a given style factor if all three presidents at one extreme, but none of those at the other extreme, possess the trait.

In general the results of these analyses are disappointing. Since only five of the forty-four comparisons (eleven on each style factor) prove to be statistically significant, one must consider the possibility that most of the comparisons reflect only chance differences. Again the most clear-cut differentiation occurs with the intellectual presidents, who are seen as more student-oriented and more concerned with faculty and as less concerned with community relations than the nonintellectual presidents. Two of these correlations are consistent with other facts about intellectual presidents: They communicate frequently with faculty, express a good deal of concern about faculty, and spend relatively little time with potential donors. These results also suggest that, even though these intellectual presidents experience major disappointments in their faculty contacts, they are viewed by their fellow administrators as being on good terms with faculty.

The major difficulty with our analysis of these interviews is that the opinions of individual administrators are frequently contradictory. For example, one of the intellectual presidents is described as follows by five administrators: the assistant dean says that the "faculty's attitude has been changed [by the president] for the better" and the student affairs officer comments that the president "works with faculty and faculty development." The dean notes that half the faculty call him by his first name and the planning officer says the president provides input into faculty decisions. But another dean comments: "He misreads opinion. . . . Faculty lack confidence in him."

An even more extreme disagreement is illustrated by the comments of administrators in an institution with a bureaucratic president. Five administrators describe the president as remote, aloof, low-key, invisible, and out-of-touch. But an administrator in the financial aid office comments that this same president is "informal and casual; you can work with him comfortably," and the dean of a professional school describes him as "approachable." Further, the chief fiscal officer characterizes him as "open; very easy access . . . available to us."

The frequency of such inconsistencies and contradictions convinced us of two facts about presidential styles: (1) Presidents can frequently be very different things to different people; and (2) The evaluative judgments of one or even several associates may be a very unreliable source of information about the administrative performance and operating style of a college president.

*Job Satisfaction.* Are different presidential types satisfied with different aspects of their jobs? To explore this question, we utilized a section from the self-administered questionnaire in which presidents were asked to indicate their satisfaction or dissatisfaction with nineteen different aspects of their jobs. For each aspect, presidents indicated whether they were very satisfied, somewhat satisfied, or not satisfied. Six of these satisfaction items are significantly ($p < .05$) related to one or more of the presidential types.

By far the most satisfied of all the presidential types is the counselor, accounting for five of the seven significant correlations between style scores and the satisfaction items. The counselors tend to be well satisfied with job security (.54), relations with students (.48), opportunity for scholarly pursuits (.49), availability of time to spend with family (.54), and opportunity for leisure time (.51). That counselors should feel that their jobs are relatively secure is perhaps to be expected, since length of time at the institution is one of the measures used to define this type. That they also tend to be satisfied in general raises an interesting causal question: Does presidential job satisfaction come naturally as a result of being at an institution for a long time, or are the more satisfied presidents simply more likely to stay in their jobs longer? Note also that these correlations could be interpreted in terms of low scores: that is, presidents who are new on the job are most likely to experience a sense of job insecurity and to feel that they have too little time for family, leisure, or scholarly pursuits.

The two other significant correlations involved the intellectual and the egalitarian types. Intellectuals tended to be satisfied with their relations with students (.43), a finding that confirms their strong interest in academic matters and is also consistent with their being viewed by administrative colleagues as student-oriented. The final significant correlation involved the egalitarians, who tend to be satisfied with the "status of my position" (.41). Although the meaning of this correlation is not readily apparent, it may be that the egalitarians feel free to fraternize with all members of the academic community because they are not sensitive about protecting their personal status within the institution.

Three other presidential satisfaction items significantly correlate with the size of the institution. There are positive correlations between size and satisfaction with "visibility for jobs at other institutions" (.66), as well as "opportunities for different (better) jobs at this institution" (.51) and a negative one between size and satisfaction with "autonomy in decision making" (−.36). Since large institutions are more visible nationally than are small institutions (Astin and Lee, 1971), it is not surprising that presidents of large institutions should feel that their jobs make them visible outside the institution. That they also feel that they could move into a better job at the same institution may reflect the greater diversity of administrative and faculty positions characterizing most larger institutions. It must be added, however, that the president of the relatively large institution may have to trade some autonomy in decision making for these greater opportunities for mobility.

## Summary

An analysis of presidential communication patterns and of the president's operating style as perceived by others at the institution enables us to identify four presidential types: The bureaucrat, the intellectual, the egalitarian, and the counselor.

Bureaucrats operate through an inner circle comprising their immediate staff and their top vice-presidents (the chief academic and fiscal officers, in particular). They are perceived by other administrators and faculty as remote, inefficient, and ineffective. Bureaucrats are most likely to be found in large commuter institutions and least likely to be found in small, sectarian, residential colleges.

Intellectual presidents have frequent contact with faculty and are seen by their faculty and administrative colleagues as intellectual, concerned with academic issues, and student-oriented. They tend to avoid getting involved with potential donors or with community relations. They express strong concern about academic matters and tend to be satisfied with their relations with students, but their frequent contact with faculty often proves frustrating. Intellectuals are most apt to preside over selective colleges and colleges located in the Northeast and least likely to be found in midwestern colleges.

Egalitarian presidents spend much of their time interacting with a wide variety of constituents: students, faculty, low-level administrators, donors, and visitors. They are seen by their faculties and administrative colleagues as nonauthoritarian, and they feel well satisfied with their status within the institution. Egalitarians are most likely to be at midwestern institutions and least likely to be at institutions in the Northeast.

Presidents of the counselor type prefer to deal with others through personal conversations and informal meetings. They tend to be older and to have been at the institution longer than other presidential types. They are also more satisfied than the other types, particularly with their job security and their time for family, leisure, and scholarly pursuits.

# FOUR

# *Five*
# *Administrative*
# *Styles*

~~~~~~~~~~~~~~~~~~~~~~~~~~~~~~~~

Faculty, students, and other members of the academic community frequently speak of the administration or of administrators in stereotypic terms. The analysis reported in the preceding chapter, however, suggests that there are several varieties of presidential style. In this chapter we explore a set of questions relating to the administration in general: How do college administrations differ from one another? Are there identifiable types of administrations? To what extent does the general administration reflect the president's style? Are certain types of administrations more likely to be found in certain types of institutions?

The information used to identify different types of administrations comes from several items on the administrators' questionnaires: frequency of communication among different administrators and between administrators and other members of the academic community; information sources used by administrators to learn of other administrators' activities; the importance administrators place on the display of various traits by their subordinates; administrators' perceptions about whether the institution rewards the display of such traits; the percentage of working time spent by administrators on campus; the percentage of administrators who earn significant outside income; and the turnover rate among administrators.

## A Typology of Administrations

The analytical procedures used to identify different types of college administrations are very similar to the procedures used to identify types of presidents (see Chapter Three). A factor analysis was performed in which the following sixty variables were used: ten measures of how frequently administrators have personal contact with other members of the campus community (Table 10), eight measures of the administrators' sources of information about other areas of the administration (Table 11), seventeen measures of how much administrators value different behaviors in their professional subordinates (Table 12), eighteen measures of what traits administrators feel are rewarded at their institution (Table 12), three measures of other administrative characteristics (Table 13), and four measures of different presidential styles (from Chapter Three).

The variables were factored by the principal components method and rotated to orthogonal simple structure by the VARIMAX method. Because of the very small sample size ($N = 41$), the results should be interpreted with some caution.

Five identifiable types of administrations emerge from the factor analysis of the sixty administrative measures. These different types, which are discussed separately below, have been tentatively labeled as follows: hierarchical, humanistic, entrepreneurial, insecure, and task-oriented. Two of these types of administrations—the hierarchical and the humanistic—appear to directly reflect particular presidential styles.

**Table 13. Selected Background Information on Principal Administrators (N = 41 institutions)**

| | | Range of Institutional Means | |
|---|---|---|---|
| Characteristic of Administrator[a] | Mean of Institutional Means | Lowest | Highest |
| Mean years at the institution | 10.9 | 5.9 | 18.4 |
| Mean percentage of working time spent on campus | 65.6 | 12.1 | 91.7 |
| Mean percentage earning outside annual income of $5,000 or more | 15 | 0 | 43 |

[a] All administrators other than the president (mean number of respondents at each institution is six).

*The Hierarchical Administration.* The label *hierarchical* was selected to describe the type of administration in which the president is the focal point of attention and the lowest-level administrators seem to have very low status. Other adjectives which might be used to describe this type of administration are conventional, orthodox, or formalistic.

The hierarchical administration is defined by the following variables:

|  | *Factor Loading* |
|---|---|
| *Presidential style:* | |
| bureaucrat | .85 |
| *Administrators communicate frequently with:* | |
| president | .60 |
| *not* financial aid officer | −.63 |
| *not* registrar | −.51 |
| *Traits administrators value in subordinates:* | |
| *not* frankness | −.63 |
| *not* salesmanship | −.53 |
| *Administrative behavior that is rewarded:* | |
| personal ambition | .64 |

*Factor Loading*

*Length of time administrators have been
    at the institutions*                     −.40

The very high loading of a bureaucratic presidential style
(.85) suggests that hierarchical administrations and bureaucratic
presidents usually go together. Administrators in the hierarchical
administration tend to communicate frequently with the president
but infrequently with their lower-level colleagues (the financial aid
officer and the registrar). Since frequency of communication with
higher-level administrators other than the president does not load
significantly on this factor, it can be assumed that the frequency of
such communication is average in hierarchical administrations.

Administrators feel that personal ambition is rewarded in
a hierarchical administration, although as individuals they tend not
to value displays of frankness or salesmanship from their subordinates. The negative loading of mean length of time that administrators have been at the institution can be interpreted in at least
two possible ways: Administrative turnover in hierarchical administrations may be greater than average, or relatively new or inex-
perienced administrators may tend to adopt a hierarchical pattern
of operation.

*The Humanistic Administration.* The term *humanistic* was selected to describe the type of administration that is clearly people-
oriented and emphasizes personal interaction on the part of all
members of the campus community.

The humanistic administration is defined by the following
variables:

*Factor Loading*

*Administrators communicate frequently with:*
    chief academic officer              .79
    chief fiscal officer                .74
    registrar                           .64
    admissions officer                  .53
    faculty                             .51
    students                            .39

|  | *Factor Loading* |
|---|---|
| *Presidential style:* | |
| egalitarian | .80 |
| *Traits administrators value in subordinates:* | |
| *not* professional or technical | |
| competence | −.41 |
| *Administrative behaviors that are rewarded:* | |
| interpersonal skills | .56 |
| *not* competitiveness | −.51 |
| *not* influence with those in power | −.51 |
| *not* willingness to apple-polish | −.40 |
| *Sources of administrators' information* | |
| *about each other:* | |
| *not* faculty | −.49 |

The high loading of the egalitarian presidential style on this factor (.80) suggests that most egalitarian presidents are associated with humanistic administrations. Perhaps the outstanding behavioral feature of the humanistic administration is that administrators frequently interact on a personal basis with each other as well as with faculty and students. These results suggest strongly that egalitarian presidents set the tone of frequent interaction with all members of the campus community and that their behavior is imitated by their administrative colleagues. At the same time, institutions with humanistic administrations may favor candidates with egalitarian values when they recruit new presidents.

It is hardly surprising that administrators in a humanistic environment feel that interpersonal skills are highly rewarded and that competitiveness, apple-polishing, and influence with those in power are not rewarded. Humanistic administrators also seem to place less emphasis on professional or technical competence in their subordinates. Finally, since humanistic administrators communicate so frequently, it is to be expected that they do not consciously rely on faculty as a source of information about each other.

*The Entrepreneurial Administration.* The entrepreneurial administration is characterized by the following variables:

|                                                    | *Factor Loading* |
|----------------------------------------------------|:----------------:|
| *Traits administrators value in subordinates:*     |                  |
| aggressiveness                                     | .76              |
| risk taking                                        | .69              |
| competitiveness                                    | .46              |
| interpersonal skills                               | .54              |
| *Administrative behaviors that are rewarded:*      |                  |
| aggressiveness                                     | .58              |
| frankness                                          | .57              |
| risk taking                                        | .39              |
| *not* scholarship                                  | −.44             |
| *Presidential style:*                              |                  |
| *not* intellectual                                 | −.53             |
| *Administrators make $5,000 or more in outside income* | .55          |

In the entrepreneurial administration, administrators value the same traits in their subordinates that they feel are generally rewarded in the institution: aggressiveness and risk taking. They also value competitiveness and interpersonal skills in their subordinates and believe that the display of frankness among administrators is rewarded. This combination of traits, coupled with the finding that the administrators at such institutions tend to make a good deal of outside income, prompted our decision to label this type *entrepreneurial.*

Entrepreneurial administrations tend not to have intellectual presidents and not to reward the display of scholarship. This pattern tends to reinforce the notion that entrepreneurs and risk takers have relatively little interest in intellectual and scholarly matters.

*The Insecure Administration.* The insecure administration is characterized by the following variables:

|                                                | *Factor Loading* |
|------------------------------------------------|:----------------:|
| *Traits administrators value in subordinates:* |                  |
| willingness to apple-polish                    | .64              |

|  | *Factor Loading* |
|---|---|
| salesmanship | .40 |
| *not* creativity | −.66 |
| *not* effectiveness in dealing with students | −.56 |

*Administrative behaviors that are rewarded:*

| nepotism or "buddyism" | .76 |
|---|---|
| willingness to apple-polish | .66 |
| *not* effectiveness in dealing with students | −.67 |
| *not* initiative | −.51 |
| *not* support from faculty | −.45 |
| *not* cooperativeness | −.41 |

*Sources of administrators' information about each other:*

| formal reports | .64 |
|---|---|
| through the faculty | .61 |
| gossip, hearsay, or through the grapevine | .36 |

*Administrators communicate frequently with:*

| visitors | .50 |
|---|---|
| students | .43 |

*Presidential style:*

| intellectual | .43 |
|---|---|

We experienced some difficulty in interpreting this pattern of results because it is the only presidential or administrative factor with clearly negative features.

Many of the items suggest that a suspicious tone and lack of trust characterize these institutions. But the high factor loading of nepotism or "buddyism" as a behavior that is rewarded by administrators suggests a kind of cronyism where administrators dispense special favors to selected friends. We finally settled on the term *insecure* for several reasons. First, the factor loading of apple-polishing as a trait that is valued and rewarded suggests an undue susceptibility to flattery. Moreover, an insecure administrator might well feel threatened by colleagues or subordinates who display the traits that show negative loadings: initiative, cooperativeness, effectiveness with students, and faculty support. Finally, administrators who are insecure in their positions would be expected to seek information about their administrative colleagues through indirect sources such as formal reports, faculty, and gossip.

It is difficult to explain why administrators in an insecure environment tend to communicate relatively frequently with visitors and students. Is it possible that they are seeking information from any available source outside the administration? Do frequent contacts with visitors and students enhance their feelings of security? Or does the generally negative atmosphere prompt them to seek gratification outside their regular administrative responsibilities?

One final comment concerns the moderately positive loading of the intellectual presidential style. While any interpretation of this finding must be highly speculative, one possible explanation involves the intellectual president's strong identification with faculty: Could it be that the intellectual president, perhaps unconsciously, creates a sense of insecurity by communicating contempt for career administrators? Or does the president who is strongly committed to faculty interests generate mistrust among fellow administrators because "he is one of theirs, not ours"?

*The Task-Oriented Administration.* The fifth type, the task-oriented administration, is defined by the following variables:

|  | Factor Loading |
|---|---|
| *Traits administrators value in subordinates:* | |
| support from faculty | .76 |
| scholarship | .66 |
| initiative | .63 |
| influence with those in power | .58 |
| willingness to accept authority | .56 |
| willingness to apple-polish | .52 |
| cooperation | .50 |

|                                                | *Factor Loading* |
| *Administrative behaviors that are rewarded:*  |                  |
| initiative                                     | .66              |
| creativity                                     | .67              |
| professional or technical                      |                  |
| competence                                     | .57              |
| cooperation                                    | .47              |
| aggressiveness                                 | .44              |

The project staff proposed a number of labels for this type: functionalist, competent, effective, responsible, mature, faculty-oriented, and instrumentalist. We chose *task-oriented* because virtually every trait that defines this type seems relevant to effective administration. Perhaps the only exceptions are the value placed on apple-polishing and aggressiveness, but both have relatively small factor loadings. We also feel that task-oriented describes the two traits which are both valued and rewarded: initiative and cooperation.

What is particularly puzzling about this type is that the intellectual presidential style does not have a significant factor loading, even though support from faculty is apparently regarded as the most important trait for administrative subordinates to display. Apparently, administrations that value faculty support as important to successful performance are not necessarily the same administrations that are likely to be headed by presidents who strongly identify with the faculty.

## Correlates of Administrative Type

Are particular types of administrations likely to be found in particular types of institutions? Are administrators more likely to be satisfied with their jobs if their administration is of one type rather than another? To explore these questions, we first computed for each institution five "scores" corresponding to each of the five types of administration. Like the four presidential style scores, the five administration type scores consist of a weighted combination of the highest-loading items listed in the preceding section under each administrative type.* These scores reflect how closely any institution's administration resembles each of the five hypothetical types. For example, an institution's administration receives a high score on the hierarchical type if the administrators communicate frequently with the president but infrequently with the registrar and financial aid officer, if the administrators feel that personal ambition is rewarded in the institution but they themselves do not value frankness and salesmanship in their subordinates, and if the administrators have been at the institution for a relatively brief time. These five administrative type scores were then correlated with measures of administrator satisfaction and institutional characteristics. Results of these analyses are summarized below.

Of the forty-one administrations considered, twenty-eight have scores on one or more of the styles which are at least half a standard deviation above the mean. There are six humanistic, six insecure, four entrepreneurial, three task-oriented, and two hierarchical administrations. Those with mixed styles include two that are hierarchical-entrepreneurial and one each that are humanistic–task-oriented, insecure–task oriented and humanistic-entrepreneurial. Two administrations display mixtures of three styles: insecure-hierarchical-entrepreneurial and insecure-humanistic–task-oriented.

*Administrator Satisfaction.* How satisfied are the administrators in our sample with various aspects of their jobs? Table 14 summarizes their average level of satisfaction with nineteen different job characteristics. To arrive at the means shown in the table, we first computed a mean score on each of the job characteristics separately for each of the forty-one institutions and we then computed the mean of these means.

*Each high-loading item was first converted into a standard score (mean = 0; standard deviation = 1) and then weighted and summed arithmetically to obtain the administrative type score. Items with negative loadings were weighted by −1. All other items were given weights of +1, except the presidential type scores, which were omitted from the computation of administrative type scores in order to keep the two sets of scores independent.

Table 14. **Mean Satisfaction of Administrators with Various Aspects of Their Jobs**

| Characteristic of Administrators'[a] Job | Mean of Institutional Means[b] |
|---|---|
| Responsibility | 2.86 |
| Variety in activities | 2.83 |
| Challenge | 2.82 |
| Congenial work relationships | 2.78 |
| Job security | 2.62 |
| Autonomy | 2.61 |
| Competency of colleagues | 2.61 |
| Relations with students | 2.58 |
| Power | 2.57 |
| Influence | 2.56 |
| Status of position | 2.55 |
| Fringe benefits | 2.50 |
| Status of the institution | 2.47 |
| Visibility for jobs at other institutions | 2.37 |
| Salary | 2.26 |
| Opportunities for different (better) jobs at the institution | 2.06 |
| Availability of time to spend with family | 1.96 |
| Opportunity for scholarly pursuits | 1.93 |
| Opportunity for leisure time | 1.84 |

[a] All administrators except the president.
[b] The administrators' responses are expressed numerically according to the following scale: very satisfied = 3; somewhat satisfied = 2; and not satisfied = 1.

The administrators in most institutions express a high degree of satisfaction with responsibility, variety in activities, challenge, and congenial work relationships. They are only somewhat satisfied, however, with salary, opportunities for better jobs at their colleges, opportunity for scholarly pursuits, and time for leisure and family. One gets the impression of a group of industrious individuals who find their work interesting and challenging but who feel somewhat overworked and underpaid.

When these nineteen measures of mean satisfaction are correlated with each of the five administrative type scores, a number of statistically significant correlations emerge. Table 15 shows the results of these correlational analyses for those thirteen administrator satisfaction measures that have one or more statistically significant correlations with administrative styles. Administrators in a hierarchical environment tend to feel relatively dissatisfied with their relations with students, job security, and opportunities for better jobs at their institutions. The hierarchical administration has negative correlations with all but one of the nineteen satisfaction measures, the median correlation being −.20. (The majority of these correlations are not shown in Table 15 because they are not statistically significant.) Although only three of these eighteen negative correlations are statistically significant, it seems likely that many of them would turn out to be so if a more sensitive test could be attained with a larger sample of institutions. The negative correlation with opportunities for better jobs at the institution suggests that administrators in a hierarchical administration feel locked into their jobs.

The humanistic administration is significantly correlated with half the satisfaction measures (nine of nineteen). Moreover, all but one of the ten remaining measures are positively correlated, with a median correlation of .22 for all nineteen measures. That satisfaction with congenial work relationships is the highest correlation (.63) confirms the notion that the humanistic administration is strongly person-oriented. Apparently, a humanistic administration has a very positive atmosphere where administrators feel well satisfied with almost every aspect of their jobs.

The entrepreneurial administration produces significant positive correlations with two areas of satisfaction: challenge and opportunities for different (better) jobs at the same institution. This type of administration is positively correlated with thirteen of the nineteen satisfaction measures, with a median correlation of .10. Given that entrepreneurial administrations reward traits such as aggressiveness, risk taking, and competitiveness, it is hardly surprising that people in such environments tend to feel that their jobs are highly challenging.

The insecure administration is negatively correlated with two satisfaction areas: congenial work relationships and variety in activities. Considering the atmosphere of mistrust that permeates the insecure administration, it is hardly surprising that administra-

**Table 15. Correlations Between Type of Administration and Mean Satisfaction of Administrators.**

| Area of Administrator[a] Satisfaction | Type of Administration | | | | |
|---|---|---|---|---|---|
| | Hierarchical | Humanistic | Entrepreneurial | Insecure | Task-Oriented |
| Responsibility | | | | | |
| Variety in activities | | .42 | .55 | -.37 | |
| Challenge | | | | | |
| Congenial work relationships | | .63 | | -.37 | |
| Autonomy | | .51 | | | |
| Job security | -.39 | .42 | | | .58 |
| Influence | | .41 | | | |
| Relations with students | -.41 | | | | .37 |
| Power | | .51 | | | |
| Status of position | | .51 | | | .47 |
| Fringe benefits | | .58 | | | |
| Opportunities for different (better) jobs at the institution | -.37 | | .37 | | |
| Opportunity for leisure time | | .38 | | | |

*Note:* Only statistically significant ($p < .05$) correlation coefficients are shown.

[a] All administrators except the president.

tors in this type of environment tend to feel that their work relationships are not particularly congenial. The insecure administration is negatively correlated with eighteen of the nineteen satisfaction measures, with a median correlation of −.17.

The task-oriented administration is positively and significantly correlated with three areas of satisfaction: job security, relations with students, and status of position. In addition, the task-oriented administration is positively correlated with all nineteen satisfaction measures, with a median correlation of .14. In short, administrators in a task-oriented administration seem to feel comfortable and secure in their jobs. One possible interpretation is that, because the administrative reward structure is focused primarily on the successful completion of each administrator's assigned responsibilities, administrators know what is expected of them and thus find it easier to develop a sense of security and status.

The nineteen satisfaction measures also produce several significant correlations with institutional characteristics that merit brief discussion. Perhaps the most interesting result is the substantial negative correlation (−.69) between the selectivity of the institution and the administrators' satisfaction with their relationships with students. At least two different explanations of this result are possible. First, since brighter students tend to be more critical and verbally aggressive (Astin, 1968), students in selective institutions may be more likely to criticize or otherwise take issue with administrative policy. Second, since faculty tend to have more power and autonomy in the more selective institutions, students may perceive administrators in such institutions as subordinates who simply cater to faculty interests. Several other significant correlations between satisfaction and institutional characteristics involve the regional measures. Administrators in southern institutions are significantly less satisfied with salaries ($r = -.41$), a finding which may reflect the generally lower cost of living that is characteristic of many southern states. The administrators in midwestern institutions report greater satisfaction with variety in activities ($r = .54$), whereas administrators in eastern institutions report greater dissatisfaction with opportunities for better jobs at their college ($r = -.51$). This latter finding may reflect the greater competitiveness of institutions in that region. Finally, administrators at institutions in the West are more satisfied ($r = .44$) with availability of time to spend with family, a result that suggests the more casual and relaxed lifestyle associated with that region.

*Institutional Characteristics.* The five types of administration have only a few significant correlations with the seventeen institutional characteristics (see Chapter Three). Institutional size proves to be negatively related ($-.46$) with the humanistic administration, a finding which supports the notion that the environments of larger institutions tend to be more impersonal. Size is positively related to the hierarchical administration, although the coefficient ($.35$) just fails to reach statistical significance. This latter result is consistent with the finding that size is positively related to the bureaucratic presidential type (see Chapter Three). Protestant institutions, as would be expected from their smaller size, produce the reverse pattern of relationships: Protestant control correlates .37 with the humanistic administration and $-.40$ with the hierarchical administration.

One somewhat puzzling relationship involves the negative correlation ($-.42$) between the entrepreneurial administration and the affluence of the institution, as measured by its per-student expenditures for educational and general purposes. Why the less affluent institutions should have more entrepreneurial climates is not immediately apparent. One possibility is that the administrators in the poorer institutions encourage more entrepreneurial activity (including earning outside income) than those in the richer institutions.

The only other significant correlation with institutional characteristics involves two regional measures: insecure administrations are likely to be found in southern institutions ($.51$), and entrepreneurial administrations are likely to be found in midwestern institutions ($.50$). Two other correlations with regional characteristics just fail to reach the significant level of confidence: hierarchical administrations are likely to be found in the East ($.36$), and task-oriented administrations are likely to be found in the West ($.35$).

## Summary

Our analysis of sixty different measures of college administrations has enabled us to identify five different types of administrations: hierarchical, humanistic, entrepreneurial, insecure, and task-oriented.

Hierarchical administrations directly reflect a bureaucratic presidential style. Administrators tend to focus their attention on the president, whereas lower-level administrators are left out of the communication network. Hierarchical administrations reward those administrators who are personally ambitious, and discourage displays of frankness or salesmanship. Hierarchical administrations are generally associated with dissatisfaction among administrators, particularly with respect to their sense of personal status, job security, and opportunities for advancement. Hierarchical administrations are most characteristic of larger institutions and those whose administrators have been employed for a relatively short time.

Humanistic administrations reflect the presence of an egalitarian president. Administrators at all levels communicate frequently with each other, as well as with faculty and students. The reward structure favors interpersonal skills over such traits as competitiveness, apple-polishing, and influence with those in power. The humanistic administration is more strongly associated with satisfaction among administrators than is any other type. They are especially well satisfied with their work relationships, fringe benefits, and sense of security, of personal status, of power, and of influence. Humanistic administrations are most likely to be found in small institutions.

The entrepreneurial administration is characterized primarily by a system that rewards traits such as aggressiveness, risk taking, competitiveness, and frankness. Entrepreneurial administrations are seldom headed by intellectual presidents. The administrators in this type of environment are likely to make a substantial amount of outside income. Entrepreneurial administrations are most likely to be found in the Midwest and in institutions that are relatively poor.

The insecure administration is characterized by an atmosphere that rewards apple-polishing, nepotism or "buddyism," and salesmanship, but does not value such administrator traits as effectiveness in dealing with students, creativity, initiative, and faculty support. Administrators in this environment tend to be dissatisfied with their jobs and to rely on indirect sources of information about each other. This type of administration is often headed by an intellectual president. Insecure administrations are most likely to be found in institutions located in the southern states.

The fifth type, the task-oriented administration, emphasizes traits such as initiative, cooperation, professional or technical competence, scholarship, and support from faculty. Administrators in this environment tend to be well satisfied with their jobs, particularly with respect to job security and sense of personal status.

# FIVE

# *Leadership's Impact on Faculty*

~~~~~~~~~~~~~~~~~~~~~~~~~~~~~~~~~~~~

In the two preceding chapters, four presidential styles and five types of college administrations were identified. This chapter considers how these administrative variables are related to several outcomes pertaining to faculty: behavior, satisfaction with administrative services, and job satisfaction. In addition, it explores the relation between faculty outcomes and other characteristics of the institution.

## Faculty Behavior

The analyses of faculty behavior are based on the thirty-five institutions at which twenty or more faculty responded to the faculty questionnaires. Eight measures of faculty behavior at each institution were constructed from these questionnaires. Table 16 shows the means and the highest and lowest institutional scores on each of the eight measures. The first measure, number of years that the faculty respondents have been at the institution, is presented as an estimate of faculty turnover. The second measure—whether the faculty member has performed administrative work during the three years prior to the survey—serves as an indication of the extent to which the administration involves faculty directly in administrative tasks. However, the high mean score and the extraordinary range of scores suggest that faculty respondents may have interpreted the term *administrative work* very broadly to cover more than just those activities normally assigned to administrators. In all likelihood, many faculty members considered meetings, committee work, and other normal faculty activities in their responses to this question.

The third behavioral measure in Table 16 is the proportion of faculty who earned at least $5,000 in outside income; this measure provides a rough estimate of the faculty's involvement in external professional activities. Once again, the variation from institution to institution is considerable: from a low of 10 percent to a high of 55 percent.

**Table 16. Measures of Faculty Behavior (*N* = 35 institutions)**

| Behavioral Measure | Mean of Institutional Means | Range of Institutional Means | |
|---|---|---|---|
| | | Lowest | Highest |
| Years at the institution | 9.5 | 5 | 13 |
| Percentage of faculty who performed administrative work in the last three years | 49.9 | 14 | 100 |
| Percentage of faculty earning at least $5,000 in outside income | 23.3 | 10 | 55 |
| Mean percentage of working time spent in: | | | |
| teaching | 58.4 | 38 | 71 |
| research and scholarship | 15.2 | 3 | 30 |
| professional activities | 9.7 | 5 | 17 |
| committees | 9.7 | 6 | 16 |
| other administrative tasks | 21.3 | 10 | 47 |

The last five items in Table 16 concern the faculty's allocation of working time to various tasks. Not surprisingly, since these
are faculty members at liberal arts colleges, the task which takes up
most of their time is teaching. At the typical institution, faculty devote about 58 percent of their time to this activity, although at a
number of institutions in the sample, the faculty spend less than
half their working time teaching. What is somewhat surprising is
the relatively large amount of time that these faculty members
spend in committee work and other administrative tasks. At the
typical institution, faculty members spend about twice as much time
on such activities (31 percent) as they do in carrying out research or
scholarly work (15 percent).

Are any of these behavioral measures related to the style of
the president or the type of administration at the institution? As
Table 17 shows, seven of the nine administrative variables developed in Chapters Three and Four are significantly related to one or
more of the eight behavioral measures.

One of the most interesting patterns of relationships involves the bureaucratic presidential style. At institutions where the
president is a bureaucrat, faculty members tend to be heavily involved in administrative tasks and to spend relatively little time
teaching. These findings are open to several interpretations that
have potentially important implications for policy. For example, it
may be that bureaucratic presidents require faculty to expend a
considerable amount of time and energy on such activities as writ-
ing reports and attending meetings. Further, these activities may
consume time that faculty would otherwise devote to teaching. At a
more general level, these findings suggest that teaching time may
be sacrificed if faculty are required to engage in a wide range of
administrative activities. Such a conclusion is consistent with Blau's
(1973) finding of a negative relationship between highly bureaucratic organizational styles and teaching quality (see Chapter One).

That the presence of an intellectual president on the campus
is associated with the faculty's spending a relatively large amount of
time on scholarly activities is perhaps to be expected, given the intellectual's strong interest in academic matters. But the negative

**Table 17. Significant Relationships Between Faculty Behavior and Administrative Variables (*N* = 28 institutions)**

| | | | Faculty Behavior | | | |
| | | | *Percentage of Time Spent in* | | | |
| *Administrative Variable* | *Years at This Institution* | *Performed Administrative Work Recently* | *Teaching* | *Research and Scholarship* | *Committee Work* | *Administrative Work Other than Committees* |
|---|---|---|---|---|---|---|
| *Presidential style:* | | | | | | |
| bureaucrat | -.48 | .39 | -.47 | | | .41 |
| intellectual | | | | .34 | | |
| egalitarian | | | | | | |
| counselor | | | | | -.34 | |
| *Type of administration:* | | | | | | |
| hierarchical | | | -.42 | | | |
| humanistic | | | | | | |
| entrepreneurial | | | | -.37 | | |
| insecure | -.46 | | | | | |
| task-oriented | | | .35 | -.45 | | |

*Note:* Only statistically significant ($p < .05$) correlation coefficients are shown.

relationship ($r = -.48$) between the intellectual presidential style and the average number of years that the faculty have been at the institution is surprising. Why should a high faculty turnover rate be associated with the presence of an intellectual president? Some interesting speculations suggest themselves: Perhaps intellectual presidents foster a publish-or-perish atmosphere at the institution whereby young faculty members are evaluated according to rather stringent standards, leading to a high turnover rate. It could also be that by neglecting financial and other institutional exigencies, some intellectual presidents indirectly cause faculty uneasiness, particularly in the small financially troubled liberal arts colleges. Still another possibility is that faculty dissatisfaction leads to a high turnover rate, and this causes trustees to hire intellectual presidents (who will presumably cater to faculty interests). Whatever the explanation, this result clearly merits further analysis.

The final significant correlation involving presidential style is a negative relationship between the amount of time spent by faculty in committee work and the presence of a counselor president. Since presidents with this style tend to operate on a very personal and informal level, they may prefer to dispense with formal committees whenever possible.

The hierarchical administration, like the bureaucratic presidential style, is associated with the faculty's devoting relatively little time to teaching. This type of administration is also positively associated with time spent in administrative work other than committees, but the coefficient does not reach statistical significance ($r = .27$). Two types of administrations—the entrepreneurial and the task-oriented—are both associated with a reduction in the amount of time faculty devote to research or scholarly activities. The task-oriented administration is also related to a higher percentage of time faculty devote to teaching, a finding which suggests that this type of administration encourages a trade-off in faculty effort that favors teaching over research. The humanistic administration is also associated with increased teaching time, but the coefficient ($r = .30$) barely fails to reach significance ($.05 < p < .08$).

The final significant relationship presented in Table 17 suggests that an insecure type of administration, like an intellectual president, is associated with increased faculty turnover.

Six of the eight behavioral measures are also related to other characteristics of the institution. Mean length of time at the institution, for example, is positively associated (.58) with colleges in the Midwest, and negatively associated (−.38) with those in the West. Apparently, faculty turnover rates are high in the West and below average in the Midwest.

The proportion of faculty members who earn at least $5,000 in outside income is positively related (.50) to the urbanity of the institution and negatively related (−.37) to its residential emphasis. The most likely explanation here is that faculty who work in institutions located near or in urban centers have many more opportunities to make outside income than do those who work at rural colleges. Urbanity and residential emphasis also appear to be involved in a trade-off between administrative work and teaching. The college's urbanity is positively associated (.34) with faculty time spent in other administrative work and negatively associated (−.37) with time spent in teaching. The opposite pattern is found for the residential emphasis measure, which correlates −.41 with time spent in other administrative work and .34 with time spent teaching. These findings suggest that, at rural institutions where a large proportion of the students live in campus housing, faculty devote considerable time to teaching and relatively little to administrative work.

Several other administrative characteristics are involved in a trade-off between research and teaching. Faculty at large institutions spend relatively more time performing research (.55) and relatively less teaching (−.49). Similarly, faculty at colleges located in the East show a relatively great commitment to research (.56) and relatively little to teaching (−.34), as do faculty at nondenominational institutions (a correlation of .67 with time spent in research and of −.41 with time spent in teaching). Also tending to spend more time in research are faculty at selective institutions (.34) and at institutions with a relatively high rate of expenditures per student (.33). These last two correlations support the stereotype that selective and affluent institutions place considerable emphasis on faculty research activities.

### Satisfaction with Administrative Services

The faculty questionnaire includes a section in which the respondent is asked: "How satisfactory are support services in the following areas: typing, budgeting, research assistance, and administrative assistance?" The response categories are very satisfactory, somewhat satisfactory, or not satisfactory. Table 18 shows the mean proportions of faculty members who are very satisfied with each of the four administrative services. They are much more likely to be satisfied with budgeting and administrative assistance than with typing and research assistance, but the range of institutional scores on all four of these measures is remarkable: For each of the four, there is at least one institution where virtually every faculty member completing the questionnaire feels very satisfied; conversely, there are several institutions where fewer than half feel satisfied. Indeed, virtually no faculty members at some institutions report being very satisfied with typing and research assistance.

Are these satisfaction measures related to the four presidential styles or the five types of administration? Our analyses show

**Table 18. Faculty Satisfaction with Administrative Services ($N = 28$ institutions)**

| Service | Mean of Institutional Means[a] | Range of Institutional Means | |
|---|---|---|---|
| | | Lowest | Highest |
| Typing | 46.6 | 0 | 100 |
| Budgeting | 74.0 | 40 | 100 |
| Research assistance | 49.4 | 0 | 98 |
| Administrative assistance | 73.7 | 33 | 100 |

[a] Percentage of faculty who are very satisfied with the service.

that the bureaucratic presidential style is negatively related to satisfaction with the quality of administrative assistance (−.59), as well as to satisfaction with typing (−.32) and budgeting (−.32). (The last two correlations just fail to reach significance.) It seems that the presence of a bureaucratic president interferes with efficient delivery of administrative services to the faculty, although in theory bureaucratic control should facilitate delivery of these practical services. Perhaps the officers in a bureaucratic system are so concerned with protecting their own domains that their interactions with others are more adversary than facilitative.

The only other significant correlation between presidential style and the four administrative service variables involves the intellectual presidential style, which is positively associated with satisfaction with the quality of research assistance. This finding once again confirms the intellectual president's strong interest in and support of faculty research and scholarship.

Only one of the five administrative types is significantly correlated with quality of administrative services, but the results are striking. The entrepreneurial administration is strongly related to dissatisfaction with budgeting (−.52), research assistance (−.58), and administrative assistance (−.51). A simplistic interpretation of this result is that the administrators in the entrepreneurial environment are so busy competing for power and earning outside income that they neglect their responsibility to provide basic support services for faculty. However, one might also argue that entrepreneurial administrators are likely to harness their energies into raising resources for the college and that the dissatisfaction of the faculty is a result of their disagreement with administrators who discount faculty support in favor of other institutional priorities.

Measures of faculty satisfaction with administrative services also produce some interesting correlations with institutional variables. Faculty satisfaction with the quality of research assistance is positively related (.52) to institutional affluence (per-student expenditures for educational and general purposes) as well as to the residential emphasis measure (.39). These results suggest that the quality of research assistance for faculty may depend to some ex-

tent on the institution's resources for hiring assistants and on the
ready availability of prospective student employees.

Institutional size is negatively related to satisfaction with
budgetary services (−.41) and with administrative assistance
(−.42), a finding consistent with the negative relationship between
a bureaucratic presidential style and satisfaction with administrative services (discussed above). Controlling for institutional size by
means of partial correlational analyses does not, however, fully account for these negative relationships involving the bureaucratic
style. In other words, independent of institutional size, the bureaucratic presidential style seems directly related to the quality of administrative assistance provided to the faculty.

## Job Satisfaction

Faculty job satisfaction was assessed by means of the same set
of items used to assess job satisfaction among administrators (see
Chapter Four). Table 19 shows the mean percentage of faculty
members who say they are very satisfied with each of nineteen
aspects of their jobs. By far the most satisfactory area is that of
relations with students: More than three fourths of the faculty at a
typical institution report that they are very satisfied. At several institutions, all faculty members report being very satisfied, and at no
institution are fewer than three in five faculty members very
satisfied. The next two aspects of the job that give the greatest satisfaction are congenial work relationships and responsibility: About
three in five faculty members report that they are very satisfied in
these areas.

Those aspects of the job producing the greatest degree of
dissatisfaction among faculty are salary, opportunity for scholarly
pursuits, opportunities for better jobs at their home institution, and
visibility for jobs at other institutions. At not a single one of these
thirty-seven institutions are more than one third of the faculty very
satisfied with their salaries—a remarkably low rate even considering the relatively low salary scales at most private colleges ("Administrators' Salaries . . .," 1979, p. 6). The small proportion expressing

Table 19. Faculty Satisfaction with Various Aspects of Their Jobs
(*N* = 37 institutions)

| Characteristic of Job | Mean of Institutional Means[a] | Range of Institutional Means | |
|---|---|---|---|
| | | Lowest | Highest |
| Relations with students | 77.8 | 65 | 100 |
| Congenial work relationships | 62.0 | 45 | 85 |
| Responsibility | 60.1 | 43 | 70 |
| Challenge | 54.8 | 38 | 68 |
| Variety in activities | 51.5 | 38 | 65 |
| Competency of colleagues | 48.0 | 34 | 65 |
| Job security | 47.7 | 25 | 68 |
| Status of position | 44.1 | 29 | 61 |
| Autonomy in decision making | 41.3 | 24 | 65 |
| Fringe benefits | 38.5 | 4 | 65 |
| Status of the institution | 32.8 | 7 | 70 |
| Influence | 30.9 | 17 | 50 |
| Power | 29.6 | 17 | 52 |
| Availability of time to spend with family | 26.4 | 10 | 36 |
| Opportunity for leisure time | 21.8 | 5 | 35 |
| Opportunity for scholarly pursuits | 20.8 | 5 | 45 |
| Opportunities for different (better) jobs at the institution | 20.8 | 5 | 35 |
| Salary | 17.5 | 2 | 34 |
| Visibility for jobs at other institutions | 15.5 | 7 | 41 |

[a] Percentage of faculty reporting they are very satisfied with the characteristic.

satisfaction with opportunity for scholarly pursuits probably reflects the strong teaching emphasis and the general lack of resources for research activities at most liberal arts colleges. That faculty are also rather pessimistic about their chances for getting better jobs (either at their own institutions or at other institutions) is understandable in view of the poor academic job market of the mid 1970s: Many faculty probably feel locked into their positions at these small colleges.

A comparison of the ranking of job satisfaction areas for faculty (Table 19) and for administrators (Table 14) suggests that

faculty and administrators in these institutions tend to be satisfied
or dissatisfied with the same job aspects. The greatest area of disagreement is relations with students—the number one satisfaction
area for faculty but only number eight for administrators. Faculty
are also somewhat more satisfied than administrators with their
opportunities for leisure time and with the availability of time to
spend with their families, whereas administrators are more satisfied
with their power and with their visibility for jobs at other institutions.

Is faculty satisfaction related to presidential style? Table 20
shows the significant correlations between the four presidential
styles and the nineteen satisfaction measures. All four of the presidential style measures produce three or more significant correlations with satisfaction measures, and all but five of the nineteen
satisfaction measures yield at least one significant correlation with
the presidential style measures.

The bureaucratic presidential style is significantly correlated
with eight job satisfaction measures, more than any of the other
presidential styles. With one exception, these correlations are all
negative—consistent with the AAHE-NEA Task Force report discussed in Chapter One—which strongly suggests that the presence
of a bureaucratic president on the campus is associated with general faculty dissatisfaction. In fact, sixteen of the nineteen correlations between the job satisfaction measures and the bureaucratic
presidential style are negative, with a median correlation of $-.28$.
The seven measures with negative correlations shown in Table 20
suggest that, at institutions with bureaucratic presidents, the faculty
feel insecure, bored, and powerless. Satisfaction with opportunities
for leisure time, however, is relatively high at such institutions;
perhaps the otherwise negative consequences of a bureaucratic re-
gime prompt many faculty members to seek their satisfaction in
outside leisure activities.

The intellectual presidential style is significantly correlated
with three job satisfaction measures: opportunities for scholarly
pursuits (positive), fringe benefits (negative), and salary (negative).
The first of these is consistent with other evidence suggesting that

**Table 20. Significant Relationships Between Presidential Style and Faculty Job Satisfaction (N = 28 institutions)**

| Area of Satisfaction | Presidential Style | | | |
|---|---|---|---|---|
| | Bureaucratic | Intellectual | Egalitarian | Counselor |
| Relations with students | -.38 | | | .34 |
| Congenial work relationships | | | | |
| Responsibility | -.46 | | | .40 |
| Challenge | -.50 | | | .38 |
| Variety in activities | | | | |
| Competency of colleagues | -.36 | | | |
| Job security | -.38 | | | |
| Status of position | | | | |
| Autonomy in decision making | -.43 | | | |
| Fringe benefits | | -.40 | .35 | |
| Status of the institution | | | | |
| Influence | -.36 | | .37 | |
| Power | | | .37 | |
| Availability of time to spend with family | | | | |
| Opportunity for leisure time | .46 | | | .37 |
| Opportunity for scholarly pursuits | | .38 | | .36 |
| Opportunities for different (better) jobs at the institution | | | | |
| Salary | | -.37 | | |
| Visibility for jobs at other institutions | | | | .38 |

*Note:* Only statistically significant ($p < .05$) correlation coefficients are shown.

intellectual presidents are strongly supportive of the faculty's scholarly interests, but why such presidents should also be associated with faculty dissatisfaction over salary and fringe benefits is not immediately apparent. A possible interpretation is that the strong emphasis on scholarly pursuits encourages many faculty members to develop unusually high aspirations for material rewards. Or it may be that the more competitive hiring practices of research-oriented universities have this same effect. As mentioned previously, intellectual presidents may deemphasize practical issues with the result that faculty believe their salaries and benefits would be improved if greater attention were paid to financial management. Whatever the explanation, the results suggest that one consequence of having an intellectual president is that the faculty will eventually become dissatisfied with their salaries and fringe benefits. In passing, it should be noted that the presence of an intellectual president is generally associated with faculty dissatisfaction: thirteen of the nineteen measures are negatively (although not significantly) correlated with this presidential style.

The egalitarian presidential style, in contrast, is generally associated with faculty satisfaction. Although only three of the correlations are statistically significant, fourteen of the nineteen coefficients are positive, and the median correlation is .14. The democratic approach that characterizes the egalitarian president is related to feelings of power and influence on the part of the faculty.

The presidential style of counselor is also strongly associated with faculty satisfaction. All but one of the nineteen coefficients are positive, the median correlation being .28, and six reach statistical significance. At colleges with a counselor as president, the faculty tend to be satisfied both with intrinsic job characteristics (challenge, responsibility, and student relations) and with more peripheral kinds of rewards (time with family, time for leisure, and visibility for other jobs). While it is not easy to interpret these findings, perhaps the counselor's very informal and personal style creates an atmosphere in which faculty develop a generally positive attitude toward their work. Also, the counselor's own strong sense of job satisfaction (Chapter Three) may be contagious. It may well be that counselor presidents prevail on campuses with seasoned administrations, campus stability, and balanced budgets. The causal relationships are difficult to interpret with this presidential style, but the correlations clearly merit much more intensive analysis.

How are these nineteen measures of faculty satisfaction related to the five types of administration? Table 21 shows the significant correlations. The hierarchical administration is positively correlated with two satisfaction measures (salary and competency of colleagues) and negatively correlated with one (relations with students). Only this last correlation is consistent with the results for the bureaucratic presidential style. Since the hierarchical administration in large part reflects the presence of a bureaucratic president, it is of some interest that the two administrative measures produce such different results. Apparently, with respect to faculty dissatisfaction, a bureaucratic president seems to be a more important factor than a hierarchical administration.

At colleges with a humanistic administration, faculty tend to be satisfied with their influence and their relations with students but dissatisfied with their opportunity for leisure time. The positive correlation with influence is consistent with the results for the egalitarian president, and that with student relations is consistent with the positive (though statistically nonsignificant) relationship discussed earlier between the humanistic administration and the time faculty devote to teaching. One possible interpretation of the negative result with leisure time is that faculty members in a humanistic environment have less time for leisure activities because they are deeply involved in their professorial activities.

By far the largest number of significant correlations with administrative type involve the entrepreneurial administration. Fifteen of the nineteen job satisfaction measures are negatively correlated with this administrative type, and six of these correlations reach statistical significance. Apparently, faculty at institutions with an entrepreneurial administration are generally dissatisfied with their jobs. The substantial negative correlation ($-.52$) with satisfaction with opportunities for scholarly pursuits is consistent with two

**Table 21. Significant Relationships Between Type of Administration and Faculty Job Satisfaction ($N = 28$ institutions)**

| Area of Satisfaction | Type of Administration | | | | |
|---|---|---|---|---|---|
| | Hierarchical | Humanistic | Entrepreneurial | Insecure | Task-Oriented |
| Relations with students | -.39 | .37 | | | |
| Congenial work relationships | | | | | |
| Responsibility | | | -.35 | | |
| Challenge | | | -.46 | | |
| Variety in activities | | | -.38 | | |
| Competency of colleagues | .39 | | | | |
| Job security | | | | | |
| Status of position | | | | | |
| Autonomy in decision making | | | -.48 | | |
| Fringe benefits | | | | | |
| Status of the institution | | .41 | | | |
| Influence | | | | | |
| Power | | | | | |
| Availability of time to spend with family | | | | | |
| Opportunity for leisure time | | -.40 | -.52 | | |
| Opportunity for scholarly pursuits | | | | | |
| Opportunities for different (better) jobs at the institution | | | | | .39 |
| Salary | .35 | | | -.44 | |
| Visibility for jobs at other institutions | | | -.35 | | .35 |

*Note:* Only statistically significant ($p < .05$) correlation coefficients are shown.

other findings reported earlier: that in colleges with an entrepreneurial administration, faculty tend to spend relatively little time in research activities and to be dissatisfied with the quality of the research assistance that they receive.

The insecure administration is negatively correlated with fourteen of the nineteen satisfaction measures, but only one of these coefficients (with salary) reaches statistical significance. The task-oriented administration, in contrast, is positively associated with fourteen of the nineteen satisfaction measures. Apparently, at institutions with a task-oriented administration, faculty tend to be well satisfied with their prospects for other jobs, both at their home institution and at other institutions.

A number of other institutional characteristics are associated with the faculty's degree of satisfaction about various aspects of their jobs. By far the most notable is the residential emphasis measure, which is significantly and positively correlated with twelve of the nineteen job satisfaction measures. The strongest correlations are with satisfaction over status of the institution (.59), status of the position (.56), autonomy in decision making (.44), and responsibility (.40), but residential emphasis is also significantly correlated with faculty satisfaction about fringe benefits, variety in activities, power, congenial work relationships, competency of colleagues, opportunities for advancement within the institution, relations with students, and job security. It seems that faculty members in residential colleges are generally more content than are those in commuter colleges.

The job satisfaction measures are also positively related to several measures of institutional quality and affluence. Thus, faculty members in selective institutions with high tuitions and large per-student expenditures are generally satisfied with their jobs, and especially with their autonomy in decision making, status of the institution, competency of colleges, variety of activities, power, and responsibility. In effect, faculty members in the more selective and affluent institutions believe that their institutions have high status, hold their colleagues in high regard, and see themselves as being autonomous.

An opposite pattern of relationships is found with respect to institutional size. That is, faculty members at relatively large institutions tend to be dissatisfied with their relations with students (−.50), influence (−.35), and responsibility (−.34). In addition, those at predominantly black colleges are dissatisfied with job security, responsibility, power, influence, variety in activities, and autonomy. In contrast, faculty members in women's colleges find their jobs relatively satisfying, as is evidenced by the substantial correlations between this institutional type and satisfaction with status of position (.63), job security (.49), autonomy (.53), and relations with students (.37).

The job satisfaction measures are also related to some extent to geographical region. Thus, faculty members in southern institutions are likely to be dissatisfied with salary (−.38), influence (−.32), and job security (−.32); those in midwestern institutions are likely to be satisfied with their salaries (.40), and those in western institutions tend not to think highly of the competence of their colleagues (−.39).

## Summary

In this chapter we have examined the relation between faculty behavior and satisfaction, on the one hand, and administrative characteristics, on the other. The principal findings for each presidential style and for each type of administration are summarized below.

At colleges with a bureaucratic president, faculty members tend to spend a relatively large amount of time in administrative activities and relatively little time in teaching. They are likely to be dissatisfied with the quality of the administrative services that they receive and indeed with most aspects of their work, in particular, with the challenge, autonomy, and responsibility of their jobs. This dissatisfaction with the intrinsic aspects of the job may lead them to seek satisfaction in outside leisure activities, the only area which is positively associated with the bureaucratic presidential style.

The presence of an intellectual president on campus seems to have its greatest impact on the faculty in the area of research and scholarship. At colleges with an intellectual president, the faculty devote a relatively large amount of their time to research and tend to be very satisfied with the quality of research assistance and with opportunities for scholarly pursuits. They are likely to be dissatisfied, however, with their salaries and fringe benefits. Finally, colleges with intellectual presidents have relatively high faculty turnover rates.

Egalitarian presidents are associated with a relatively high degree of faculty satisfaction, particularly with their sense of power and influence. The data also suggest that the presence of an egalitarian president may lead to increased faculty involvement in teaching.

The counselor is more strongly associated with faculty satisfaction than any other presidential style. Faculty who serve under such presidents seem to be more satisfied than average with both the intrinsic and the extrinsic aspects of their jobs.

At institutions where a hierarchical administration prevails, faculty devote relatively little time to teaching and tend to be dissatisfied about their relations with students. They are, however, more satisfied than average with the competence of their colleagues and with their salaries. This last finding may be attributable primarily to the dominance of hierarchical administrations at the larger institutions (which pay better salaries than do small institutions).

Like the egalitarian presidential style, the humanistic administration is associated with the faculty's feeling satisfied with their influence and with their relations with students. At institutions with humanistic administrations, however, faculty are likely to be dissatisfied with their opportunities for leisure.

Faculty serving under an entrepreneurial administration devote relatively little time to research and scholarship and tend to be generally dissatisfied with most aspects of their jobs. In particular, they are likely to be dissatisfied with administrative services and such job features as challenge, variety in activities, responsibility, autonomy, and opportunity for scholarly pursuits.

The insecure administration is associated with faculty dissatisfaction over salaries and with high faculty turnover rates.

At institutions where the administration is of the task-oriented type, faculty devote comparatively little time to research and scholarship but considerable time to teaching. Moreover, the faculty tend to be satisfied with most aspects of their jobs, especially with job opportunities within the institution and at other institutions.

# SIX

# *Leadership's Impact on Students*

~~~~~~~~~~~~~~~~~~~~~~~~~~~~~~~~

Do students perceive and react to different administrative patterns of behavior? Are they affected by the president's style or the administrative structure and procedures at an institution? Can any empirical relationships be established between administrative variables and measures of student behavior and attitudes? This chapter explores these questions by first reviewing interview data and then relating the nine measures of presidential style and administrative type (Chapters Three and Four) to a number of student outcome measures.

## Student Perceptions

As was mentioned in Chapter One, group interviews were conducted with some of the student leaders at a number of the institutions in the sample. Among the questions raised are two that relate directly to students' perceptions of the administration: (1) How much say do students have in general administrative decisions? and (2) Do you think the administration does a good job?

Before statistically testing our theory that administrative variables affect even the distal student outcomes, we examined the responses of the student interviewees to these items by institution, attempting to relate these responses qualitatively to the dominant presidential style or administrative type at the institution.

The results are encouraging. For instance, in the one institution with an extremely low score on humanistic administration and a very high score on insecure administration, the responses of the students participating in the group interview are summarized by the interviewer as follows: "The students have no power. The administrators are phantoms." One student leader at an institution with a high score on hierarchical administration comments: "Students feel they have little effect. The administration does a good job running the college." Student comments from two institutions with highly humanistic administrations are: "They are constantly asking for feedback"; and "You can walk in and talk to the administration; they listen." Equally striking are comments made by student leaders attending institutions with highly insecure administrations: "Students come and go but the administration stays, is the attitude "; and "Students sit on most committees but don't think they are listened to." Finally, a student from an institution with a task-oriented administration says that "They do a good job, but I wish they took a more personal leadership."

Since the discussion questions were framed in terms of the overall administration, the student leaders had little to say about the presidents. Three students made specific references to the president, however. The following is a comment about a president whose style is strongly bureaucratic: "He's a photo for the average student; they don't see him." Of a president who embodies the intellectual style, one student states that "The new president may have a lot to do with changes in the student role in decision making." One president who scores very low on the intellectual measures is described as follows: "The president isn't a scholar but a businessman."

Obviously, such qualitative observations are not conclusive, but they do suggest that students, though removed from the administration, sometimes perceive and react to identifiable administrative structures and styles. This lends credence to our belief that administrative effects on student attitudinal and behavioral outcomes can be measured.

Because the administration can, in theory at least, affect the student in a variety of ways, the student questionnaire includes a diverse set of student outcome measures. These measures fall into two broad categories: outcomes related to administrative services and outcomes related to the student's adjustment to college life.

### Administrative Services

Table 22 shows the institutional means and the highest and lowest institutional scores on thirteen diverse measures of the quality of administrative service for students. The first contact between student and administration usually comes during the application process when prospective students request application forms, catalogues, financial aid forms, and other information about the institution. The student questionnaire contains an item which inquires, "Prior to your enrollment, how quickly did the information (catalogue, application, financial aid) you requested from the college arrive?" Students were asked to respond on a five-point scale from "very slowly" (score 1) to "very quickly" (score 5). The first item in Table 22 indicates the proportion of students who checked points 4 or 5 on this scale. About two thirds of the students at the typical institution feel that the response to their request for information was rapid, although the range across institutions is substantial (from 20 percent to 83 percent).

The next major administrative procedures experienced by the student are orientation, registration, and the allocation of student housing assignments. Four items in Table 22 relate to these services: the usefulness of information given at orientation, any complications in housing assignments, the number of hours required to register, and enrollment in all of first-choice classes. Again, institutions vary widely in the quality of these services.

**Table 22. Quality of Administrative Services for Students** ($N = 37$ institutions)

| Service | Mean of Institutional Means | Range of Institutional Means | |
|---|---|---|---|
| | | Lowest | Highest |
| Speed of response to student's initial request for information (catalogue, application, financial aid) | 65.5[a] | 20 | 83 |
| Usefulness of information given at orientation | 50.4[b] | 22 | 73 |
| Complications in housing at arrival on campus | 19.3[c] | 0 | 52 |
| Hours required to register | 3 | 1 | 16 |
| Enrollment in all of first-choice classes | 54.1 | 6 | 97 |
| Classroom space adequate | 70.5[c] | 45 | 92 |
| Laboratory facilities adequate | 79.1[c] | 34 | 96 |
| Adequacy of contacts with financial aid officer: | | | |
| Data readily available | 84.3[c] | 0 | 100 |
| Data accurate | 82.7[c] | 50 | 100 |
| Data complete | 78.7[c] | 33 | 100 |
| Student was confident about what to expect on arrival at college | 39.7[d] | 22 | 56 |
| Reality turned out to be consistent with expectations | 34.1[d] | 13 | 52 |
| Administration concerned about and interested in the needs of students | 89.0[e] | 55 | 100 |

[a] Percentage of students marking 4 or 5 on a five-point scale from "very quickly" (5) to "very slowly" (1).

[b] Percentage marking 4 or 5 on a five-point scale from "very useful" (5) to "not useful" (1).

[c] Percentage marking "yes."

[d] Percentage marking 4 or 5 on a five-point scale from "strongly agree" (5) to "strongly disagree" (1).

[e] Percentage responding "a great deal" or "moderately" (compared to "not at all").

The next two items in Table 22 concern the adequacy of physical facilities. Satisfaction with classroom space and laboratory facilities generally runs high, although at some institutions fewer than half the students feel that such facilities are adequate. Several additional questionnaire items (not shown in Table 22) ask students to rate their college residences on eight different characteristics: privacy, quiet for studying, lounges or sitting areas, room size, bathroom facilities, heat, student freedom, and programming (lectures, films, and the like). Results with respect to these items are mentioned later where pertinent.

Two items in Table 22—involving the student's expectations about college prior to matriculation—are included on the grounds that one of the most difficult but important administrative tasks is to give students a sense of what the college is actually like before they get there. Student expectations are affected by a number of administrative processes and products: for example, catalogues and other printed material, letters to students prior to matriculation, and responses to telephone inquiries. The data suggest that many students were not adequately prepared for college life, and it must be concluded that the administrations of most institutions fail to fulfill this important function.

The final item in Table 22 shows the results for a direct question about the student's overall perception of the administration: "Is the administration of your institution concerned about and interested in the needs of students?" The response alternatives were "a great deal," "moderately," and "not at all." At the typical institution, close to nine in ten students checked the first or second alternative, although the range across institutions is considerable (from 55 percent to 100 percent). Somewhat more variation on this question might have been achieved if the *moderately* and *not at all* alternatives had been combined, but our intention was to isolate those students who clearly believe that the administration is not student-oriented.

Another set of student outcome measures also deals with the adequacy of administrative services. Specifically, students were asked to rate eleven services on a four-point scale: very satisfactory, somewhat satisfactory, not satisfactory, and not applicable or not familiar with it. (Students selecting this last category were excluded when each satisfaction measure was computed.) Table 23 shows the proportions of students indicating that each of these eleven ad-

**Table 23. Student Satisfaction with Administrative Services and Procedures**

| Area of Satisfaction | Mean of Institutional Means[a] | Range of Institutional Means | |
|---|---|---|---|
| | | Lowest | Highest |
| Orientation | 81.0 | 44 | 97 |
| Registration | 75.8 | 22 | 97 |
| Distribution of grade reports | 75.0 | 37 | 100 |
| Curriculum advisement | 71.6 | 50 | 85 |
| On-campus housing | 61.6 | 15 | 91 |
| Health services | 55.5 | 18 | 87 |
| Financial aid | 53.1 | 21 | 82 |
| Career counseling | 50.0 | 32 | 76 |
| Distribution of transcripts | 49.2 | 35 | 69 |
| Personal counseling | 43.9 | 24 | 71 |
| Employment placement | 37.8 | 15 | 73 |

[a] Percentage rating service either "very satisfactory" or "somewhat satisfactory" (as opposed to "not satisfactory").

ministrative services or procedures is either very satisfactory or somewhat satisfactory. Students seem to be most satisfied with orientation, registration, and the distribution of grade reports; these are procedures which usually are completely routinized. They are least satisfied with employment placement and personal counseling, services which are more individualized or which require some student initiative.

*Impact of Presidential Style.* How do these twenty-four measures of the perceived quality of administrative services (Table 22) and of student satisfaction with administrative services (Table 23) relate to the administrative style of the president? As Table 24 indicates, thirteen of the twenty-four measures produce one or more significant correlations with three of the four measures of presidential style. Apparently, a college's having an intellectual president has no effect on the perceived quality of administrative services to students.

The bureaucratic presidential style is significantly correlated with seven different measures, always in a negative direction. The

**Table 24. Significant Relationships Between Presidential Style and Student Ratings of Administrative Services and Procedures**

| Administrative Service or Procedure | Presidential Style | | | |
|---|---|---|---|---|
| | Bureaucratic | Intellectual | Egalitarian | Counselor |
| Speed of response to student's initial request for information | −.44 | | | |
| Accuracy of financial aid data | −.35 | | | |
| Student was confident of precollege expectations | | | .39 | |
| Precollege expectations were fulfilled | | | .47 | |
| Administration is concerned about students | −.34 | | .48 | |
| *Satisfactoriness of:* | | | | |
| Registration | −.46 | | | |
| Financial aid | −.36 | | | |
| Curriculum advisement | −.36 | | .36 | |
| Career counseling | | | | .34 |
| Personal counseling | | | | .39 |
| Health services | | | | .33 |
| Employment placement | | | | .38 |
| On-campus housing | −.39 | | | |

*Note:* Only statistically significant ($p < .05$) correlation coefficients are shown.

presence of a bureaucratic president is associated with delays in responding to students' requests for information, inaccurate financial aid data, and dissatisfaction with registration, financial aid, curriculum advisement, and housing. Support for this last finding comes from further correlations between the bureaucratic presidential style and low student ratings of the adequacy of dormitory room size ($-.40$), bathroom facilities ($-.41$), and quiet for studying ($-.37$). Finally, students at institutions with a bureaucratic president tend to feel that the administration is not concerned about student needs.

The egalitarian presidential style has a very different pattern of correlations with this type of student outcome. Students at institutions with an egalitarian president report that they are confident about what to expect upon arriving at college, that these expectations have been fulfilled, and that they are satisfied with the quality of curriculum advising. Not surprisingly, these students also feel that the administration is concerned about their needs.

The counselor presidential style is associated with still another pattern of student outcomes. Students at institutions with this type of president tend to be well satisfied with the quality of career counseling, personal counseling, employment placement, and health services. Since the counselor president is characterized by a preference for dealing with others on a direct one-to-one basis, it is interesting that each of these four types of services ordinarily involves similar personal contact between the student and a staff member. It may well be that counselor presidents emphasize high-quality personal services of this type and that their typically long tenure at the institution gives them ample time to build such student services.

*Impact of Administrative Type.* Does the type of administration affect the quality of administrative services for students? As Table 25 shows, ten of the twenty-four student outcome measures prove to be significantly correlated with one or more measures of administrative type, although none is significantly correlated with the insecure type of administration and only one—satisfaction with distribution of transcripts—has a significant (positive) correlation with the entrepreneurial type of administration.

**Table 25. Significant Relationships Between Type of Administration and Student Ratings of Administrative Services and Procedures**

| | Type of Administration | | | | |
|---|---|---|---|---|---|
| | Hierarchical | Humanistic | Entrepreneurial | Insecure | Task-Oriented |
| Usefulness of information given at orientation | −.44 | | | | |
| Student was confident of precollege expectations | | .59 | | | |
| Precollege expectations were fulfilled | | .63 | | | |
| Administration is concerned about students | | .48 | | | |
| *Satisfactoriness of:* | | | | | |
| distribution of transcripts | | | .44 | | |
| financial aid | −.50 | .59 | | | |
| curriculum advisement | −.39 | .48 | | | |
| personal counseling | | | | | .44 |
| health services | | | | | .42 |
| employment placement | | | | | .37 |

*Note:* Only statistically significant ($p < .05$) correlation coefficients are shown.

The hierarchical administration, like the bureaucratic presidential style that often accompanies it, is generally related to student dissatisfaction with administrative services and procedures. Specifically, at institutions with a hierarchical administration, students tend to say that the information given at orientation was not useful and to express dissatisfaction with financial aid and with curriculum advisement. The likely explanation here is that bureaucratic presidents and hierarchical administrations take a very impersonal approach to various administrative tasks, including the provision of student services. Since the president and his inner circle are isolated from other administrators, it may well be that no mechanism exists for evaluating and improving student services, which are usually under the control of middle managers and other lower-level administrators. This situation may be partially attributable to the fact that bureaucratic presidents and hierarchical administrations are more likely to be found in larger institutions. When institutional size and other characteristics are controlled, these negative correlations between student satisfaction with administrative services and the presence of bureaucratic presidents and hierarchical administrations decrease; they do not, however, vanish entirely.

The humanistic administration produces a very different pattern of results, one that closely resembles the pattern found for the egalitarian president (Table 24). Students at colleges with humanistic administrations report having a clear-cut idea of what to expect upon arriving at college and feel that these expectations have been fulfilled. They are also well satisfied with the quality of financial aid services and curriculum advisement, and they believe that the humanistic administration is generally concerned with their needs. These findings clearly confirm the impression that the humanistic administration is very people-oriented. Apparently, such an orientation results in better services and promotes a more positive student attitude toward the administration. Virtually none of these correlations shrink to nonsignificance when other institutional characteristics such as the size, selectivity, and residential emphasis of the institution are controlled, indicating that these student outcomes may be causally connected with the presence of a humanistic administration.

The pattern of significant relationships for the task-oriented administration is very similar to that for the counselor president. Thus, at institutions with such an administration, students express satisfaction with personal counseling, health services, and employment placement. While the reason for these associations is not entirely clear, one possibility is that, because task-oriented administrators emphasize the effective performance of their duties, the delivery of this type of personalized student service is likely to be superior.

*Other Institutional Characteristics.* A number of other institutional characteristics prove to be significantly related to some of the measures of student satisfaction with administrative services and procedures. For instance, at colleges scoring high on the residential emphasis measure, students are likely to express satisfaction with orientation (.66), registration (.41), distribution of grade reports (.52), curriculum advisement (.38), health services (.56), and on-campus housing (.71). Colleges scoring high on the urbanity measure show a similar pattern of relationships, except that the coefficients tend to be smaller and the correlations are all negative: In other words, at colleges located in or near large cities, students tend to be dissatisfied with these services.

Institutional size is negatively associated with student satisfaction with administrative services, although the list is somewhat different than the list associated with urbanity and residential emphasis. Generally, the larger the institution, the less likely the students are to be satisfied with the quality of personal counseling (−.41), career counseling (−.39), curriculum advisement (−.38), on-campus housing (−.44), and availability of financial aid data (−.42). In addition, students at large institutions are likely to say that residence facilities are inadequate in four respects: lounges, room size, bathroom facilities, and programming such as lectures and films.

The selectivity of the institution produces a mixed pattern of correlations with the student satisfaction measures. Students in selective institutions tend to be well satisfied with registration (.44), distribution of grade reports (.48), adequacy of classroom space (.36), adequacy of laboratory facilities (.52), accuracy of financial aid data (.37), completeness of financial aid data (.35), and a number of characteristics of residence halls: privacy, quiet for studying, room size, bathroom facilities, and student freedom. On the other hand, they tend to be dissatisfied with personal counseling (−.50) and career counseling (−.44). One must be cautious in interpreting relationships with college selectivity, however, since they may represent student rather than institutional effects. For instance, a tendency to be dissatisfied with counseling services may be a characteristic of highly able students rather than an outcome of attending a highly selective institution. Such ambiguities can be resolved only through additional longitudinal research.

Students at institutions with relatively high per-student expenditures for educational and general purposes are likely to be satisfied with on-campus housing (.53), health services (.45), orientation (.38), and availability of financial aid (.36). The most probable explanation is that the more affluent institutions can afford higher-quality services in certain areas, especially housing, health services, and financial aid.

The geographical region in which an institution is located bears some relation to the satisfaction of its students with various administrative services and procedures. Thus, at institutions in the West, students tend to express satisfaction with personal counseling (.66), career counseling (.63), employment placement (.42), and distribution of transcripts (.45). At those located in the East, students tend to be dissatisfied with curriculum advisement (−.51) and to be satisfied with the amount of freedom they have in their college residences.

Students at institutions with a Protestant affiliation, in contrast, are likely to express dissatisfaction with the amount of freedom they have in their college residences; no doubt this dissatisfaction stems from the continuing *in loco parentis* policy at some Protestant institutions.

As already mentioned, statistical control of these other institutional variables reduces somewhat the relationship between the bureaucratic presidential style and several of the outcome measures. It seems that the connection between student dissatisfaction and this presidential style is partly, but not entirely, accounted for by the presence of bureaucratic presidents in the larger and less selective colleges whose students commute rather than live on campus. It should be added, however, that even after the other significant institutional characteristics are controlled, several of the negative correlations persist and that virtually all the correlations with the egalitarian president and the humanistic administration are unaffected.

## Student Adjustment

The degree to which students were able to adjust to various aspects of their college experience was assessed by means of the following question: "How difficult did you find each of the following in your adjustment to college?" Students were asked to respond on a three point scale: very difficult, somewhat difficult, and not difficult. As Table 26 indicates, of the eight different adjustment areas assessed, the three presenting the greatest adjustment difficulties are in academic areas: studying efficiently, earning satisfactory grades, and managing time (this last item is highly correlated with the first two items). Students most easily adjusted to being away from home and to meeting and knowing other students. Institutional variation in the extent to which students experienced these difficulties depends in part on the area in question. For example, the proportions of students who experienced difficulty in studying efficiently and in managing time is about the same from one institution to another: a mean of 77 percent, with a range of only about 25 percentage points between the lowest-scoring and the highest-scoring institution. Institutions vary considerably, however, in terms of the proportions of their students who had problems earning satisfactory grades, getting to know

**Table 26. Student Difficulties in Adjustment**

| Area of Difficulty | Mean of Institutional Means[a] | Range of Institutional Means | |
|---|---|---|---|
| | | Lowest | Highest |
| Studying efficiently | 76.8 | 61 | 85 |
| Managing time | 75.9 | 61 | 87 |
| Earning satisfactory grades | 70.1 | 33 | 88 |
| Living within a budget | 64.0 | 44 | 78 |
| Getting to know faculty members | 59.9 | 31 | 77 |
| Selecting a major field of study or a career | 51.5 | 38 | 69 |
| Meeting and knowing other students of both sexes | 50.8 | 31 | 81 |
| Being away from home and friends | 41.0 | 24 | 63 |

[a] Percentage responding *very difficult* or *somewhat difficult* (as opposed to *not difficult*) in response to the question "How difficult did you find each of the following in your adjustment to college?"

faculty members, or meeting other students; the range from lowest-scoring to highest-scoring institutions on these items is about 50 percentage points.

*Impact of Administrative Characteristics.* Are the difficulties that students have in adjusting to college life related to the president's operating style or the institution's administrative type? As Table 27 indicates, seven of the eight adjustment areas (all except "earning satisfactory grades") are significantly related to one or more of the seven administrative variables. (Neither the counselor president nor the insecure administration has a discernible influence on student adjustment.) Note that a positive relationship in this table indicates adjustment difficulties, whereas a negative relationship indicates relative ease of adjustment.

With respect to studying efficiently and managing time, the pattern for the intellectual presidential style is the reverse of the pattern for the entrepreneurial administrative type. That is, at institutions with an entrepreneurial administration, students are likely to have problems studying efficiently and managing time,

**Table 27. Significant Relationships Between Administrative Variables and Student Adjustment**

| | Area of Possible Adjustment Difficulty | | | | | | |
|---|---|---|---|---|---|---|---|
| Administrative Variable | Studying Efficiently | Managing Time | Living Within Budget | Getting to Know Faculty | Selecting a Major or Career | Meeting Other Students | Being Away from Friends |
| *Presidential style:* | | | | | | | |
| bureaucratic | | | | | | | |
| intellectual | -.45 | -.41 | | | | | |
| egalitarian | | | -.42 | | | | |
| counselor | | | | -.42 | | | .47 |
| *Type of administration:* | | | | | | | |
| hierarchical | | | | | | | |
| humanistic | | | | -.40 | | | |
| entrepreneurial | .39 | .66 | | | | .39 | .42 |
| insecure | | | | | | | |
| task-oriented | .49 | .50 | .41 | | .38 | | |

*Note:* A positive correlation indicates that the administrative variable is related to difficulty in adjustment. Only statistically significant ($p < .05$) correlation coefficients are shown.

whereas at institutions with an intellectual president, they are much less likely to experience such problems. Note that the intellectual president and the entrepreneurial administration have contrasting orientations toward research and scholarship. The intellectual president emphasizes and supports research and scholarship, and is associated with faculty satisfaction with their opportunities for scholarly pursuits. In contrast, the entrepreneurial administration places relatively little emphasis on research and scholarship, and faculty members under such an administration tend to be dissatisfied with many aspects of their jobs, including opportunities for scholarly pursuits. Is it possible that administrative emphasis on faculty scholarship and research somehow influences the student's ability to manage time and to study efficiently? Do strongly research-oriented faculty give students different kinds of assignments and make different demands on them? While these interpretations are admittedly tenuous, they merit more intensive analysis in subsequent research studies where measures of more specific faculty practices could be used.

The patterns of correlations for the egalitarian president and the humanistic administration are once again very similar. Both administrative variables are associated with the student's getting to know faculty members with relative ease, a finding consistent with the personal orientation of the humanistic administration and, more particularly, with the relationship found earlier between that administrative type and faculty satisfaction with student relations (Chapter Five). Egalitarian presidents and humanistic administrations are also associated, however, with student difficulty in adjusting to being away from home and friends, although the explanation for this relationship is not readily apparent. One might suppose that such difficulties are attributable to the strong residential emphasis of the colleges, but such is not the case: None of the other institutional characteristics is significantly related to this adjustment measure. The explanation must remain a mystery until more intensive analysis is undertaken.

The pattern of correlations between the task-oriented administration and the student adjustment measures is equally puzzling. At colleges with such an administration, students are likely to have difficulty managing time, studying effectively, living within a budget, and selecting a major or a career. Since none of these correlations shrink to nonsignificance when other institutional characteristics are controlled, there must be some direct connection between the task-oriented type of administration and student difficulties in these four areas. These relationships seem to contradict the positive student ratings of personal counseling, employment placement, and health services that are associated with the task-oriented administration. Like the entrepreneurial administration, the task-oriented administration places relatively little emphasis on faculty research and scholarship, so perhaps student difficulties with managing time and studying efficiently under these two types of administration have a common explanation. Again, more research is needed to identify underlying causal relationships.

*Other Institutional Characteristics.* The institutional characteristic most strongly associated with any of the student adjustment measures is size, which correlates .77 with difficulty in getting to know faculty members. This result confirms a long-established fact: the larger the institution, the smaller the likelihood of close student-faculty contacts being established (see, for example, Astin, 1968, 1977b). Controlling for institutional size does not, however, obliterate the relationship between the egalitarian presidential style or the humanistic administration and relative ease in getting to know faculty.

At more selective institutions, students are likely to find it relatively easy to live within a budget ($-.45$) and manage their time ($-.34$) but relatively difficult to select a major or a career (.34) and to meet and know students of both sexes (.57). The last correlation may result from the greater selectivity of single-sex colleges as compared to coeducational colleges. Logically enough, attending a single-sex college is related to having difficulties meeting and knowing students of both sexes, as is attending an institution located in the East; most single-sex colleges are located in the eastern region of the country.

Because the relationship between presidential and administrative styles and student outcomes is surprisingly strong, we again emphasize that the institutional sample consists primarily of small liberal arts colleges. Probably administrators and faculty at large research universities would scoff at the suggestion that a president's style is even known to many students, let alone that it has a measurable impact on their adjustment to or satisfaction with college. On a small campus, however, the president and many of the other officers are well known to the students. They are frequently topics of conversation, and they are personally praised or blamed for many college policies and practices.

### Student Attrition

The substantial number of significant relationships between administrative styles and student satisfaction raises a further question that deserves attention: Are presidential and administrative styles similarly related to student persistence and attrition? Recent research (Astin, 1975, 1977a) suggests that one factor in student attrition is dissatisfaction with the college environment; thus, it may well be that the same administrative variables which are associated with satisfaction are also related to student persistence.

Because the student data described in the previous section are not longitudinal, it was necessary to search other sources to find data that could provide a reasonably well-controlled study of the effects of administrative style on attrition. After looking through the various longitudinal student files in the Cooperative Institutional Research Program (CIRP), we selected one which is based on a study of approximately 36,000 students as they entered college in 1961 with a follow-up study four years later (for further details, see Astin and Panos, 1969). The principal advantage of this file is that it includes data not only on attrition but also on the environments of each of the 246 institutions involved in the study. Of particular relevance to the current study is an environmental measure called *concern for the individual student*, which was one of thirty-five college environmental measures developed in an earlier study (Astin, 1968) and which is defined by negative scores on items such as

"The administration is not really very concerned about the individual student"; and "Most students are more like 'numbers in a book.'"

While this factor does not exactly reproduce any of the four administrative styles identified in the current study, we believe that the positive end resembles the egalitarian president and the humanistic administration, whereas the negative (low concern) end resembles the bureaucratic president and the hierarchical administration. Since the former two styles are associated with student satisfaction and the latter two with dissatisfaction, we were interested in determining whether this particular factor is related in a similar way to student persistence.

To explore this possibility, two stepwise multiple regression analyses were conducted using two measures of student persistence (as opposed to attrition) as dependent variables: (1) the student's having received a bachelor's degree within four years after entering college, and (2) the student's having completed four or more years of college at the time of the follow-up. The first step in the analysis was to control for the differential characteristics of the freshmen entering the 246 institutions. We thus employed some forty measures of the student's abilities, high school achievements, family background, and educational and career plans at the time of college entry in the fall of 1961. After controlling these background characteristics, partial correlations between the persistence measures and the environmental measure, concern for the individual student, were computed.

The results clearly confirm our expectations: The partial correlation between persistence and concern for the individual student is .38 for both measures of persistence. Not surprisingly, the enrollment size of the institution is also significantly related to the two dependent variables ($r = -.22$ for completion of four years of college and $r = -.28$ for attainment of the bachelor's degree). Since controlling for size does not reduce to nonsignificance the partial correlation with concern for the individual student, however, the effect of this environmental measure on student persistence cannot be attributed solely to the tendency of smaller colleges to have warmer and more concerned environments than large colleges.

In summary, if the environmental measure used in these special studies can be assumed to reflect, at least in part, similar administrative styles to those identified in the current study, it seems reasonable to conclude that presidential and administrative styles can have a significant impact on student persistence.

### Summary

In this chapter we identified a number of relationships between an institution's administrative characteristics and two types of student outcomes: satisfaction with administrative services and adjustment to college life. While the number and strength of these relationships surprise us, the reader should remember that we are dealing here with relatively small private institutions rather than large and complex universities. If presidential and administrative styles can make a difference for faculty and students, the private college is precisely the type of institution where one should be able to demonstrate such relationships.

The major findings are summarized below for each presidential style and type of administration.

The bureaucratic presidential style is generally associated with student dissatisfaction over administrative services and procedures. Students attending colleges headed by bureaucratic presidents tend to be dissatisfied with the registration process, financial aid services, curriculum advisement, and the quality of housing on campus and to report that the institution was slow in responding to their requests for information during the application process. Moreover, they are inclined to feel that the administration is not concerned about their needs. However, they experience little difficulty living within a budget.

The presence of an egalitarian president on campus is associated with a very different pattern of student outcomes. Students at institutions headed by egalitarian presidents believe that the administration is interested in their individual needs. They experience little difficulty in getting to know faculty and are well satisfied with the quality of curriculum advisement. They also report that they knew what to expect before arriving on campus and that these expectations were confirmed once they had enrolled. Students at such institutions, however, find it difficult to adjust to being away from family and friends.

Intellectual and counselor presidents are associated with a very limited number of student outcomes. Students attending institutions with intellectual presidents learn with relative ease how to manage their time and to study efficiently. Students attending colleges with counselor presidents are well satisfied with the quality of career counseling, personal counseling, health services, and employment placement.

The hierarchical administration, like the bureaucratic presidential style with which it is closely associated, generates student dissatisfaction. Students at institutions with hierarchical administrations are dissatisfied with the quality of curriculum advisement and financial aid services and say that the information dispensed during freshman orientation was of limited value. They also experience difficulties in meeting and getting to know other students.

The pattern of results for the humanistic administration closely resembles that for the egalitarian president. Students attending institutions with humanistic administrations believe that the administration is concerned with their welfare. They had a clear idea of what to expect before they arrived on campus, and their expectations were largely confirmed. They express satisfaction with the quality of financial aid services and curriculum advisement. Though they find it difficult to adjust to being away from family and friends, they get to know faculty members fairly easily.

The task-oriented administration is associated with both favorable and unfavorable student outcomes. On the one hand, the students at institutions with such an administration are satisfied with such administrative services as personal counseling, employment placement, and health services. On the other hand, they find it difficult to live within a budget, manage their time, study efficiently, and select a major and a career.

The insecure administration is associated with none of the student outcome measures, and the entrepreneurial administration with only three: satisfaction with distribution of transcripts, and adjustment difficulties in managing time and in studying efficiently.

The student outcomes associated with the bureaucratic presidential style and the hierarchical administration are partly, but not entirely, attributable to the fact that these administrative variables are characteristic of the larger and less selective institutions that have substantial commuter populations. The relationships found for the egalitarian presidential style and the humanistic administration, however, remain largely unaffected when other institutional characteristics are controlled.

# SEVEN

# *Implications for*
# *Practice*

~~~~~~~~~~~~~~~~~~~~~~~~~~~~~~~~~~~~

The research described in the preceding chapters concerned the description and classification of different presidential and administrative styles, and a determination of how these administrative characteristics are related to various faculty and student outcomes. In this chapter we summarize the highlights of the empirical findings and discuss the implications of these findings for administrative practice.

## Presidential Style

By analyzing data from forty-four private liberal arts colleges on how frequently the president communicates with different members of the academic community and how the president's mode of operation is perceived by others, we identified four different presidential styles: the bureaucrat, the intellectual, the egalitarian, and the counselor. The characteristics of each type and their effect on faculty and student outcomes are summarized below.

*The Bureaucrat.* Bureaucratic presidents operate through an inner circle that includes their top vice-presidents and immediate staff. Other administrators and faculty members perceive them as remote, inefficient, and ineffective. Faculty who work under bureaucratic presidents tend to spend a relatively large amount of time on administrative activities and relatively little time on teaching. They are likely to be dissatisfied with the quality of administrative services as well as with many aspects of their jobs. Students at colleges with bureaucratic presidents are also generally dissatisfied with administrative services and procedures and feel that the administration is not interested in their needs. These apparent effects of a bureaucratic president on student and faculty outcomes are attributable in part, but not entirely, to the fact that bureaucrats are most likely to preside over large commuter colleges and least likely to preside over small sectarian colleges with resident student populations.

*The Intellectual.* Intellectual presidents are oriented primarily toward the faculty. They interact frequently with faculty members and are seen by their faculty and administrative colleagues as intellectual and as concerned with academic issues. The faculty serving under intellectual presidents devote a relatively large amount of their time to research and tend to be satisfied with the quality of research assistance they receive and with their opportunities for scholarly pursuits. They are, however, likely to be dissatisfied with their salaries and fringe benefits. Despite their strong commitment to faculty, intellectual presidents are frequently frustrated in their contacts with faculty. In addition, faculty serving under intellectual presidents have a relatively high turnover rate. Students at institutions headed by intellectual presidents report little difficulty in learning how to manage time and to study efficiently, but otherwise student outcomes are generally unrelated to the presence of an intellectual president. Intellectual presidents are most likely to be found in selective colleges and colleges located in the Northeast.

*The Egalitarian.* The distinguishing characteristic of egalitarian presidents is that they spend much of their time interacting with a wide range of constituents: students, faculty, administrators at all levels, donors, and visitors. They are seen by their faculties and their administrative colleagues as nonauthoritarian and they feel well satisfied with their status within the institution. Faculty serving under egalitarian presidents tend to be satisfied with their jobs and to devote a relatively large amount of time to teaching. Students at institutions headed by egalitarian presidents feel that the administration is interested in their individual needs, have little difficulty in getting to know faculty members, and are well satisfied with their curriculum advisement. Egalitarians are most likely to preside over midwestern institutions and least likely to preside over institutions in the Northeast.

*The Counselor.* Counselor presidents are distinguished primarily by their preference for dealing with others through personal conversations and informal meetings. They are generally older and have been at their colleges longer than other presidential types. They are also more satisfied with their jobs. The counselor is more strongly associated with faculty satisfaction than is any other presidential style. In addition, students attending colleges headed by counselor presidents are well satisfied with the quality of those administrative services involving direct one-to-one contact with a staff member: career counseling, personal counseling, health services, and employment placement.

## Type of Administration

A typology of administrations was developed by means of a factor analysis of sixty measures covering the following areas of administrative behavior: the frequency with which key administrators have personal contact with each other and with other members of the campus community, their sources of information about what is happening in other areas of administration, the traits they value in their professional subordinates, the traits they feel are rewarded at their institution, and the four different presidential styles. Five different types of administrations were identified: hierarchical, humanistic, entrepreneurial, insecure, and task-oriented. The characteristics of each type and their effect on faculty and student outcomes are summarized below.

*The Hierarchical Administration.* The hierarchical administration directly reflects a bureaucratic presidential style. The attention of other administrators is focused on the president, whereas lower-level administrators are left out of the communication network. Hierarchical administrations are generally associated with dissatisfaction among all members of the academic community. Administrators are dissatisfied with their status, job security, and opportunities for advancement. Faculty feel that their relations with students are unsatisfactory and devote relatively little time to teaching. (They are, however, more satisfied than average with the competence of their colleagues and with their salaries.) Students attending institutions with hierarchical administrations are dissatisfied with the quality of orientation, curriculum advisement, and financial aid services. These relationships are attributable in part, but not entirely, to the fact that hierarchical administrations are most likely to be found in larger institutions.

*The Humanistic Administration.* The humanistic administration usually reflects the presence of an egalitarian president. Administrators at all levels communicate frequently with each other, as well as with faculty and students. The humanistic administration is associated with satisfaction among all members of the academic community. Administrators are especially satisfied with their work relationships and with their personal status, power, and influence. Faculty feel well satisfied with their influence and their relations with students. (They are, however, likely to be dissatisfied with their opportunities for leisure activities.) Students feel that the administration is concerned about their welfare and that the quality of curriculum advisement and financial aid services is high. In addition, they report that they had a clear idea of what to expect before they arrived on campus and that their expectations were largely confirmed. While humanistic administrations are most likely to be found in small institutions, the positive association between humanistic administrations and satisfaction among administrators, faculty, and students cannot be accounted for by small institutional size alone.

*The Entrepreneurial Administration.* The entrepreneurial administration is characterized primarily by a system that rewards administrators who exhibit aggressiveness, risk taking, competitiveness, and frankness. Entrepreneurial administrations are seldom headed by intellectual presidents. Administrators in this type of environment are likely to make a substantial amount of outside income and to be satisfied with their jobs. Faculty serving under an entrepreneurial administration devote relatively little time to research and tend to be dissatisfied with most aspects of their jobs. Student outcomes are not associated with this type of administration, except that students report some difficulty in learning how to budget time and study efficiently. Entrepreneurial administrations are most likely to be found at institutions in the Midwest and in institutions that are relatively poor.

*The Insecure Administration.* The insecure administration is characterized by a system that rewards apple-polishing, nepotism or "buddyism," and salesmanship on the part of administrators but does not value such traits as effectiveness with students, creativity, initiative, and faculty support. Administrators in this type of environment are dissatisfied with their jobs and rely on indirect sources of information about each other. The insecure administration, which is often headed by an intellectual president, is also associated with faculty dissatisfaction over salaries and with high faculty turnover rates. None of the student outcome measures, however, is associated with this type of administration. Insecure administrations are most likely to be found in institutions located in the South.

*The Task-Oriented Administration.* In the task-oriented administration, administrators are rewarded for displaying initiative, cooperation, professional or technical competence, scholarship, and support from faculty. Administrators tend to be well satisfied with their jobs, particularly with respect to job security and sense of personal status. Faculty at institutions with task-oriented administrations devote comparatively little time to research and scholarship but considerable time to teaching. Moreover, they tend to be satisfied with most aspects of their jobs. Students at institutions with task-oriented administrations tend to be satisfied with various administrative services, but have difficulty living within a budget, managing time, studying efficiently, and selecting a major or a career.

## Implications for Practice

At this point the reader should recall several features of the study that may limit the drawing of generalizations from the findings. First, the institutional sample comprises private liberal arts colleges, most of them relatively small and residential. While several of the institutions are large and serve substantial commuter populations, a representative sample of public institutions would surely include institutions with much larger enrollments and much larger commuter populations than the typical institution in this particular study. In addition, the inclusion of public institutions might produce different results because many public institutions operate as part of multiinstitutional systems with sources of funding and modes of governance that differ from those of the typical private college. Second, because the data are cross-sectional rather than longitudinal, any causal inferences must be highly tentative.

The following sections offer some admittedly speculative ideas, suggested by the empirical results from this study, about how to manage institutions more effectively. We have organized these ideas and suggestions into six broad categories: presidential behavior, relations among administrative colleagues, faculty relations, student relations, issues related to institutional type, and issues for further research.

*Presidential Behavior.* Many of our ideas about effective leadership relate specifically to college presidents, although we feel that the general principles summarized below can be applied as well to other top administrators. Our suggestions about presidential behavior are organized under five specific subheads: management style, effective use of time, fiscal viability, the new president, and job mobility.

Management Style. When college presidents are asked to describe the major highlights and disappointments of their administrations, they are inclined to describe their successes in terms of specific accomplishments and their failures in terms of the processes that prevented them from carrying out their plans. At the same time, they seem willing to associate themselves with specific accomplishments, but they implicitly disassociate themselves from what they regard as institutional failures. They account for these failures by citing the inability or unwillingness of others (for example, faculty) to cooperate, whereas they seldom mention the positive contributions of others to institutional successes. This pattern of findings suggests that college presidents often fail to learn from their successes because they are inclined to take them for granted. In our view, college presidents might learn to be more effective managers if they were less ready to take credit for institutional successes and more willing to share the credit with others by carefully analyzing the interpersonal and political processes that lead to successful implementation of plans and ideas.

Effective Use of Time. College presidents vary considerably in the time they devote to interacting with different constituencies. In many cases the relative time allocated to these competing groups is incongruent with the stated values and concerns of these administrators. In particular, there is reason to believe that some presidents might be able to govern more effectively if they were to interact more frequently with three groups: faculty, students, and their most valued advisors. Given this situation, it might be a useful exercise for college administrators routinely to examine their appointment calendars over a period of time to determine whether their actual time allocations are consistent with their subjective priorities.

Presidents who devote little attention to academic matters and who seldom interact with faculty might benefit from scrutinizing their motives: Is this avoidance of academic issues and faculty a rational choice among competing priorities, or is it motivated in part by a desire to avoid conflict? Does preoccupation with fund raising and other nonacademic matters merely provide a socially acceptable means to avoid involvements that will almost certainly generate a certain degree of tension and controversy?

Fiscal Viability. It seems clear that, if a private institution is to survive, it must attract and retain students. Although many college presidents and other top-ranking officials now spend considerable time and effort on fund-raising activities, they might be wiser to devote themselves to strengthening their institutions by developing a strong educational program that focuses on students' educational problems and objectives. (For specific suggestions in this area, see the section below on student relations.) In other words, the best insurance for the survival and fiscal viability of a private institution is the development of curriculums which appeal to prospective students and which are stimulating and effective enough to keep them interested after matriculation.

Results of this study suggest that students are most likely to be attracted to institutions with humanistic administrations or with presidents of the egalitarian or counselor types. The study also provides some evidence suggesting that private colleges could increase their enrollments if the president were directly involved in recruiting potential students who visit the campus. For fairly small colleges that do not have highly selective admissions policies, it might be useful to estimate the costs and benefits of such personal involvement on the part of the president. For example, for each additional student recruited by the president, the institution might realize as much as $25,000 in additional income. Even though some students might withdraw before graduation, the anticipated additional revenue would be substantial. While the institution will almost certainly incur some additional costs for additional students, these marginal cost increases are almost certain to be substantially smaller than the increases in revenue.

The New President. Presidential job satisfaction seems to be directly related to presidential longevity, and presidential longevity, in turn, seems to be associated with a style of interaction that emphasizes personal contact with others. Relatively new college presidents are frequently dissatisfied, particularly with their job security and their time for family and leisure. These results suggest a number of potentially critical questions that new college presidents might want to ask themselves: Will I tend to overwork myself because of insecurity? Is it possible that I may allow too little time for family and leisure? Is the additional productivity associated with long hours on the job worth the price of decreased time for family, leisure, and relaxation?

Job Mobility. Persons who aspire to be presidents of major institutions should be wary of accepting presidencies of very small institutions as stepping stones to more prestigious presidencies, particularly if the intermediate institution also happens to be non-selective in its admissions policy. Our study indicates that presidents of such small and nonselective institutions do not feel that their prospects for jobs at other institutions are very good. However, presidential aspirants who opt instead for a relatively large institution run a substantial risk of losing a good deal of autonomy in decision making.

*Relations Among Administrative Colleagues.* Our analyses suggest a number of potentially important relationships between the president's operating style and the behavior of other administrators. These relationships are discussed under three specific subheads: effective use of time, presidential and administrative styles, and administrative morale.

Effective Use of Administrative Time. Most institutional chief executives stand to benefit from a careful analysis of how they communicate with other administrators and how these administrators communicate with each other. Does the existing pattern of communication implicitly favor certain administrators? To what extent do critical communication links need strengthening? Are some middle management administrators (registrars and financial aid officers, for example) implicitly left out of the administrative process because of their relatively infrequent contact with administrative colleagues? Does the communication pattern suggest a hierarchical or a humanistic pattern of organization?

Presidential and Administrative Style. Our data suggest a strong connection between certain presidential and administrative styles. Specifically, bureaucratic presidents are associated with hierarchical administrations, and egalitarian presidents with humanistic administrations. Presidents who prefer a hierarchical approach, wherein most of their communications are limited to an inner circle of top vice-presidents and presidential staff, run a significant risk of increased turnover among other administrators. Presidents taking a more egalitarian approach, wherein they communicate with most principal members of the administration as well as with faculty and students, are likely to be imitated by their administrative colleagues, thereby creating a humanistic administrative environment.

Administrative Morale. High morale among members of the administration is most closely associated with a reward structure which emphasizes the successful performance of each administrator's assigned responsibilities. Apparently, this type of reward structure gives administrators a sense of job security and status.

While many college presidents believe that their principal responsibility is to the faculty, the results of this study suggest that presidents who are too closely identified with faculty may generate distrust among their fellow administrators. Presidents who are strongly committed to faculty concerns, in other words, cannot necessarily expect their administrative colleagues to share this orientation. Rather, other administrators seem to view faculty support simply as a means to accomplishing their own administrative tasks, not as a value to be shared with the president.

*Faculty Relations.* The results of this study suggest a number of potentially important considerations that administrators should take into account if they want to improve their relations with the faculty. These considerations have been organized under three specific subheads: general relations with faculty, presidential style, and type of administration.

General Relations with Faculty. For college presidents and chief academic officers, relations with the faculty represent the most severe and frequent source of conflict and frustration. Despite their important positions in the administrative hierarchy, most fiscal and development officers have very little contact with faculty and do not see faculty relations as a primary source of difficulty.

The attitudes of the president and other top administrators toward faculty can best be described as ambivalent. On the one hand, they generally have high regard for the faculty's teaching skills and ability to work with students; on the other hand, their view of the faculty's involvement in governance is usually negative and sometimes hostile. Since in most institutions faculty are involved in the decision-making process through faculty senates and institutional committees, top academic administrators must find the most effective ways to minimize negative faculty influence in the administrative process and, at the same time, in trying to solve the institution's problems, to capitalize on the faculty's particular expertise.

Perhaps the most common complaint among administrators in working with faculty is their resistance to new ideas or new proposals. Administrators often fail to recognize that many such proposals inevitably make demands on the faculty's time and energies. Given that most faculty are already extremely busy with their multiple responsibilities, they are likely to view administrative proposals for change with suspicion unless these proposals are accompanied by concrete suggestions for appropriate trade-offs in faculty time. The results of our project suggest that the most likely trade-offs can be effected in the area of administrative work. More specifically, the faculty's involvement in administrative work seems to come at the expense of the time they devote to teaching. Thus, administrative suggestions for increased effort in one of these two major areas should probably be accompanied by plans for decreased effort in the other.

Presidential Style. While the presence of an intellectual president may please those faculty who have strong research interests, this type of president is associated with faculty dissatisfaction in matters of salary and fringe benefits and with high faculty turnover rates. Egalitarian presidents are associated with increased faculty involvement in teaching, whereas bureaucratic presidents are associated with increased faculty involvement in administrative work and faculty feelings of insecurity, boredom, and powerlessness.

Type of Administration. Administrations that emphasize competition for power among administrators (for example, entrepreneurial administrations) often neglect to provide basic administrative services to faculty. In addition, administrations that are organized hierarchically appear to demand that considerable faculty time be devoted to administrative tasks.

Given the extraordinary variation from one institution to another in the degree of faculty satisfaction with different types of administrative services, institutions should periodically survey their faculty members to determine whether services such as typing, research assistance, and budgeting are being satisfactorily delivered.

*Student Relations.* Student satisfaction is greatest at institutions with egalitarian presidents and humanistic administrations and lowest at institutions with bureaucratic presidents and hierarchical administrations. These patterns suggest that communication with students is a critical factor in facilitating student development in a liberal arts college. That is, under a bureaucratic or hierarchical approach, the president is cut off from all members of the academic community except the high-ranking administrators and his or her own staff. This inner circle of top decision makers thus has no mechanism for evaluating and improving student services, which are usually under the control of middle managers and other lower-level administrators. Under a humanistic administration, in comparison, the president and other top administrators have relatively frequent contact both with students and with administrators at all levels. This latter pattern of communication seems to allow the administration to monitor students' needs and attitudes and to develop  appropriate policies and programs in response to these needs. This interpretation is supported by the fact that one other presidential type—the counselor—is also associated with student satisfaction in several areas. The counselor's outstanding characteristic, as previously noted, is a preference for direct personal communication with members of the academic community.

Considering that most of the colleges in this study are relatively small liberal arts colleges, it is remarkable that administrators at all levels so seldom seek out student advice and counsel. Administrations that wish to provide effective student services should periodically survey students to learn how they evaluate these services. Highly routinized services that are provided to all students (registration, orientation, and the like) tend to be highly rated by students at most types of institutions. Although somewhat lower ratings occur for the more individualized student services (for example, job placement and counseling), at some institutions these services are highly rated, suggesting that an institution can significantly improve its services if the administration monitors the quality of services in academic as well as nonacademic areas. (Chapter Eight outlines a proposal for how administrations can be better informed about, and more responsive to, the student's academic and nonacademic needs.)

*Issues Related to Institutional Type.* Any attempt to make college administrations more effective must be based on an awareness of the constraints that are imposed on administrative effectiveness by institutional characteristics largely beyond the control of institutional policy makers. Our analyses indicate that, in developing long-range plans to make administrations more effective, administrators should consider at least three such characteristics: size, residential emphasis, and selectivity.

Size. Perhaps the most important institutional constraints are imposed by the size and residential emphasis (see p. 142) of the institution. As already indicated, large institutions tend to have bureaucratic presidents, hierarchical administrations, and faculties who devote a good deal of time to administrative tasks and relatively little time to teaching. Small institutions, on the other hand, tend to have humanistic administrations and faculties who devote a substantial amount of time to teaching. The faculty in the small institutions also tend to be more satisfied with administrative services and with their relations with students and their influence within the institution. Since presidents at relatively large institutions are inclined to adopt bureaucratic operating styles, such presidents might find it useful to examine their own operating style from the following perspective: Do I fit the mold? Do I tend to limit my administrative contacts to my inner circle of top administrators and communicate with other constituencies primarily through my staff? Am I simply imitating the style of my predecessor or of my counterparts in other large institutions, or is there a real function or advantage to be served by adopting this particular style of operation? Are various student services adequate? Am I seen by the faculty and lower-level administrators as remote and inaccessible? What consequences might such a perception have for the morale of these administrators and faculty members? Are other operating styles better suited to my particular disposition and to the needs of this institution?

Residential Emphasis. Institutions where most of the students live on campus usually have faculties who devote a good deal of time to teaching and who are well satisfied with almost all aspects of their jobs. Institutions with substantial commuter populations, on the other hand, tend to be headed by bureaucratic presidents and to have faculties who spend more time in administrative work, less time in teaching, and a substantial amount of time earning outside income.

In certain respects, the combination of small size and strong residential emphasis provides an ideal environment for faculty to become involved in the educational process and to develop more effective relations with students (see Astin, 1977b).

Our results suggest that larger institutions and, in particular, institutions with large commuter populations have special problems of faculty and student involvement that must be addressed directly by the administration. For discussions of possible approaches to alleviating the problem of low faculty and student involvement in the commuter institution, see Astin (1975, 1977b) and Educational Facilities Laboratory (1977).

Selectivity. Highly selective colleges tend to be headed by intellectual presidents. Though faculty are generally satisfied with most aspects of their jobs, particularly salary and opportunities for research activity, they devote relatively little of their time to teaching. It seems, then, that administrations in the more selective institutions need to pay special attention to how faculty divide their time between research and teaching. While this issue will not affect nonselective colleges to the same extent, administrators in such institutions should ordinarily expect a relatively high degree of faculty job dissatisfaction.

*Issues for Further Research.* We have already suggested that virtually every relationship between administrative style and faculty or student outcomes reported in this study merits further investigation to provide more definitive tests of causal inferences. In particular, further research is needed in three areas: administrative types, their effects on students and faculty, and the evaluation and selection of administrators.

Administrative Types. The four presidential and five administrative types identified in this study by no means exhaust the typological categories that might be developed. Any typology developed by means of factor analysis is, of course, limited by the variables that enter into the original analysis. While our study makes extensive use of information on communication patterns and sources of information, we did not collect information about fiscal policies or decision-making strategies, nor did we question lower-level administrators such as assistant or associate deans. The use of such data in future typological studies might help to refine the types identified in this study, and perhaps to identify additional types not revealed here.

Our study describes the four presidential styles solely in terms of how they affect the internal operations of the institution. An important issue for future research is how effective each type is in external relations: fund raising, relations with trustees and outside constituencies, and so forth. Do bureaucrats tend to be highly successful in negotiating with coordinating boards and legislatures? Are egalitarians inept at fund raising?

Effects on Students and Faculty. We have already suggested that our cross-sectional analyses should be supplemented by longitudinal studies of changes in student and faculty outcomes under different types of administrations. Ideally one could include a number of cases in which major changes in presidential leadership or other principal administrators were introduced during the period of longitudinal data collection; in such circumstances, one could see whether the changes in administrative type or presidential style are associated with shifts in student and faculty outcomes. For example, if a bureaucratic president is replaced by an egalitarian president, will faculty and student satisfaction increase? Will the rest of the administration shift from a hierarchical to a humanistic approach? Such changes would give convincing support to the hypothesis that presidential style and administrative type are causally connected with student and faculty outcomes.

Longitudinal studies would also provide a basis for drawing more definitive conclusions about a number of provocative causal questions raised by our study:

1. Are administrators alienated by a president who caters too much to faculty needs and interests?

2. Why are intellectual presidents associated with faculty dissatisfaction over salary and fringe benefits and high faculty turnover? Does a president's strong emphasis on research and scholarship encourage faculty to develop high aspirations for material rewards? Does a publish-or-perish climate lead to high turnover rates by creating more stringent standards for evaluating young faculty?

3. Is a bureaucratic presidential style or a hierarchical administration an inevitable outcome of trying to administer the affairs of a very large institution? Is it possible to develop more decentralized structures in large institutions that will, in effect, produce a number of relatively autonomous humanistic subenvironments?

4. How can new college presidents be encouraged to avoid establishing a bureaucratic style? Are there types of institutions (large public universities, for example) where the bureaucratic style produces positive faculty and student outcomes?

5. Why is the presence of a counselor president on campus so strongly associated with faculty satisfaction? Does an informal and personal style of operation create an atmosphere in which fac-

ulty develop a positive attitude toward their work? How important is the counselor's association with faculty spending less time in administrative work?

6. Why are faculty at institutions with entrepreneurial administrations so dissatisfied with the quality of administrative services? Are the administrators in the entrepreneurial environment so busy competing with each other and earning outside income that they neglect their responsibility to provide faculty with basic support services?

7. Do egalitarian presidents, by their frequent communication with all members of the academic community as well as with low-level administrators, set an example which is followed by their administrative colleagues?

8. Can administrations become more effective by regularly surveying the needs, satisfactions, accomplishments, and problems of faculty and students?

9. Can administrators effect an increase in the amount of time faculty devote to teaching by reducing their administrative responsibilities?

10. Can presidents become more effective managers and leaders if they are encouraged to focus more closely on the processes that lead to the successful implementation of plans and ideas?

11. Can the enrollments of small institutions with declining applicant pools be increased or at least stabilized if the president becomes directly involved in recruiting students during on-campus visits?

12. Has the faculty movement for unionization and collective bargaining been accelerated by the rapid growth of community colleges? Since faculty alienation and dissatisfaction, in this study, is considerably greater in those colleges with large commuter populations than in the exclusively residential colleges, and since faculty unionization has occurred much more rapidly in commuter than in residential institutions (Baldridge and others, 1978), the recent growth in commuter institutions may well explain the rapidity of the expansion of faculty unionizing activity.

Evaluation and Selection of Administrators. The values implicit in this study suggest that the ideal way to evaluate college administrators is to determine the effects they have on fellow administrators, faculty, and students. Lacking such information, should search committees rely upon the testimonials of individual colleagues in judging the performance of administrators? Our evidence suggests that they should not. Because individual colleagues often have highly divergent views of the president, their assessments of presidential performance can be misleading unless the sample is large enough to generate a reliable consensus.

These problems in assessing administrators' performance bear directly on the question of how to select administrators. Most administrators, particularly college presidents, are selected on the basis of two kinds of information: job history (kinds of positions held) and performance during the recruiting process (appearance and interaction with search committee members). Occasionally recommendations from administrative colleagues are obtained, but these are usually few in number and subject to the kinds of distortions mentioned above. Information about student and faculty outcomes is almost never solicited.

Given the extreme variation in administrator performance and style observed in this study, we would discourage a search committee from relying on information about candidates' prior positions. One needs to know how the candidates performed, not simply what positions they held. Since information about an administrator's effect on faculty and students is usually unavailable during the search process, however, a much greater research effort is needed to determine whether the criteria currently used to select administrators are actually related to the effectiveness of later performance. This research would follow the progress of newly selected administrators and determine how they affect the rest of the college community.

# EIGHT

# *Proposals for Change in College Administration*

~~~~~~~~~~~~~~~~~~~~~~~~~~~~~~~~~~~~

Having devoted six years to this project, after some thirteen years of almost continuous research on student development, we are convinced that traditional notions about effective management in higher education need fundamental revision.

Those readers familiar with the substantial literature on student development and on college administration will probably agree that they overlap very little. Studies of student development are carried out by a very different group of researchers and read

Note: Earlier versions of this chapter were presented by A. W. Astin as a keynote address to the University of California Conference on Academic Planning for the 80s and 90s, Los Angeles, January 22–23, 1976, and included in Baird and Hartnett (1980). See also Astin, Bowen, and Chambers, 1979.

by a very different audience than studies of college administration and management. This division reflects a fundamental fact about the functioning of academic institutions. Although most institutions of higher education claim student development as a basic mission, the decision-making process in higher education typically ignores any consideration of how alternative courses of action might affect student development. This tendency is exemplified by the computer-based management information systems (MIS) now used by many colleges and universities. Analyses of these systems (Baldridge and Tierney, 1979) show that, except for simplistic information about enrollments and majors, they provide almost no information on students. Administrators who rely on such systems are thus encouraged to view planning and decision making primarily in terms of controlling costs; they place little if any weight on the probable consequences for student and faculty development.

To the student development researcher, the solution is obvious: Scrap the resource-oriented management systems and substitute systems that are primarily student-oriented. But administrators (even those sympathetic to a student-oriented approach) tend to reject this solution as unfeasible. The principal thesis of this chapter is that such a system is not only feasible but necessary if the quality of an institutions' planning and decision making is to be improved. Underlying this thesis is the assumption that every policy decision in the higher education enterprise must be based upon conceptions about how administrators and faculty operate and how students develop. The studies of college administration and student development carried out by the Higher Education Research Institute have enabled us to develop some rudimentary theories about these matters that are briefly discussed in the next two sections.

## A Theory of Administrative Behavior

As noted in Chapter One, most treatises on the theory and practice of college administration say very little about learning and education; indeed, they might as well have been written for managers of manufacturing corporations.

We feel that the principles of college administration should be drawn from a model of administration as an art form rather than as a science that can be learned by reading a how-to-do-it manual. An essential ingredient in the performing artist's development of technique and skills is the opportunity to view the results of his work. Neophyte painters see what comes out on the canvas, aspiring musicians hear what they play or sing, and adjust their behavior accordingly.

Administrators in most fields generally receive the information necessary for them to gauge the effectiveness of their efforts. For example, corporate business managers usually have access to information on sales volume and on profits and losses to guide their planning and decision making. By contrast, academic administrators—though they may have access to fiscal data—rarely receive information about student learning and development. If we accept the premise that improving the educational environment is a major objective of college administration, it follows that college administrators rarely receive appropriate information about the results of their policy. (The humanistic administration may be a notable exception to this generalization, since administrators in this environment are in frequent communication with students and faculty.) They are like artists learning to paint blindfolded or musicians learning to play the violin with their ears plugged.

The same argument can be made for college faculty and for the "performing arts" of teaching and advising. In their teaching and advising activities, faculty members probably have a better notion than do administrators about student satisfaction and discontent. But, unless faculty members systematically question all students, they are likely to hear only from the more aggressive students, the "squeaky wheels." Further, such responses do not necessarily tell the professor much about what students are actually learning. Professors might argue that their final examinations allow them to evaluate the quality of learning, but in many respects, relying on final examinations is like closing the barn door after the horse has escaped. As for advising, professors rarely have an opportunity to learn about their successes and failures in this important enterprise.

The "performing arts" analogy can be extended to support staff. Many areas of institutional functioning affect students directly: registration, orientation, financial aid, housing, food services, parking, social activities, career counseling, personal counseling, extracurricular activities, health services, and job placement. How can the personnel responsible for these diverse student services improve their programs and policies unless they solicit systematic evaluations of their efforts from the students they serve?

## A Theory of Student Development

What kinds of information about student development do administrators need? If decision makers are to develop effective short- and long-term strategies for their colleges, they must have a theory of how students learn, of what facilitates or inhibits students' educational development. The theory of student development summarized here evolved from two major studies of institutional impact on student development (see Astin, 1975, 1977b). A principal concept in the theory is that of *student involvement,* the time and the physical and psychological energy that the student invests in the academic experience. The more students are involved in the academic experience, the greater their learning and growth. The less they are involved, the less they learn and the chance increases that they will become dissatisfied and drop out.

The degree of students' involvement in the academic experience is manifested in a variety of ways: the amount of time they spend studying, the frequency of their interaction with each other or with professors, the amount of time they spend on campus, and so forth. Our longitudinal research shows that virtually every institutional policy or practice that increases involvement also enhances student development (Astin, 1977b). For example, contrary to the folklore, having a job on campus actually helps a student to stay in college. At least that is true of part-time work (fewer than twenty hours a week). When a student works more than twenty hours, the effect disappears: full-time work reverses the effect. Ideally, then, a student should have a part-time job on campus.

A second experience that enhances student learning and development (and one of the most important and pervasive effects observed in our research) is the residential experience: moving away from home and living in a college dormitory. Our present study suggests that, at institutions with a strong residential emphasis, both students and faculty are more likely to become involved in the educational process.

Belonging to a fraternal organization—a social fraternity or sorority—increases the student's persistence in college. Indeed, participation in almost any kind of extracurricular activity—an honors program, ROTC, or an undergraduate research project— enhances the student's involvement with the college, as does interacting frequently with other students, studying hard, spending a lot of time with the books, or being on an athletic team.

These research results suggest that, as a general operating principle, the administration and faculty should strive to formulate plans and policies that will encourage students to become more involved, to invest more of their time and their physical and psychic energy in the educational process.

## A Student-Oriented MIS

A student-oriented management information system would monitor student progress by regularly collecting data on involvement or any other aspect of personal development that relates to the institution's educational goals. Subsequent decisions about institutional policy and practice, including decisions about the allocation of resources, would be designed to bring about greater correspondence between student development and stated developmental goals. The system itself would be continuously subject to change through one or more of the following mechanisms: (1) redefinition of institutional objectives: adding new objectives, reordering priorities for different objectives, sharpening definitions, and so on; (2) modifications in the method of assessing particular developmental outcomes; and (3) changes in the method of analysis or in dissemination of information.

Like any MIS, the student-oriented system would be designed primarily for use in decision making. All decisions are based

on an administrator's consideration of the desired outcomes, or
*ends*, and the alternative *means* to achieve those ends. For college
administrators, the ends, of course, concern student development.
Alternative means might include organizing certain learning experiences (for example, curriculums and instructional methods),
hiring faculty or staff, structuring the physical environment (for
example, design and location of classrooms, buildings, or open
space), and establishing certain rules or regulations. Every administrative decision is predicated on the belief that some educational
outcome and the particular means selected to achieve that outcome
are causally connected. In other words, the administrator believes
that, of all the means available, the one he selects is best, because it
is most likely to produce the desired outcome.

Traditionally, college faculty and administrators have been
more concerned with means than ends. The reward structure in
higher education clearly reinforces this tendency, since administrators are rewarded not for maximizing the development of the student, but for acquiring a large share of limited resources: money,
bright students, and highly trained and prestigious faculty. The
accreditation process reinforces this concern with means, because it
seldom asks hard questions about ends.

Another reason that most administrators concentrate on
means is that the causal connections between means and ends are
not well understood. Consequently, administrators must operate
on the basis of a largely untested folklore about what works and
what does not. Thus, one major benefit of the student-oriented
MIS is that it would help administrators develop a better understanding of how their actions are likely to affect students. It would
encourage them to think more about ends than means and it would
tell them if a particular program or policy actually works.

### Student Time as a Resource

Administrators who concentrate their efforts on the acquisition of resources often fail to recognize that their greatest potential
resource may be student time. According to our theory of involve-

ment, the extent to which students achieve particular developmental goals is a direct function of the amount of time and effort they devote to activities designed to produce these gains. For example, if an improved knowledge of history is regarded as an important goal for history majors, the extent to which students reach this goal is a direct function of the time they spend listening to professors talk about history, reading books about history, discussing history with other students, and so forth. Within certain broad limits, the more time students spend in such activities, the more they learn. The time students spend taking notes at formal lectures and otherwise attempting to comprehend the material represents a fraction of the potential time and effort that they might devote to activities that contribute to their knowledge of history. The more obvious ways of increasing this time and effort are to assign out-of-class work, to improve the quality or accessibility of library offerings in history, and to make lectures and other course materials available through audiotapes and videotapes, slides, and other media. The availability of such resources, however, does not ensure that students make effective use of them. An institution may have an excellent library collection and a wealth of associated materials that students seldom use. Professors may assign homework that students fail to complete. Classes may be poorly attended, or students may attend but fail to profit significantly because they are bored or distracted. In short, an effectively managed institution not only provides appropriate learning resources but also creates an environment that encourages students to use those resources effectively. The student-oriented MIS in turn tells the administrator or faculty member whether the environment is actually having its intended effect on student involvement.

Administrators must recognize that virtually every institutional policy and practice—class schedules, policies on class attendance, regulations about academic probation and about participation in honors courses, policies about office hours for faculty, student orientation—can affect how students spend their time and how much effort they devote to academic pursuits. Moreover, administrative decisions about many nonacademic issues—the location of new buildings such as dormitories and student unions; rules governing residency; the design of recreational and living facilities; on-campus employment opportunities; number and type of extracurricular activities and regulations regarding participation; the frequency, type and cost of cultural events; roommate assignments; financial aid policies; the relative attractiveness of eating facilities on and off campus; and parking regulations—can significantly affect the way students spend their time.

## Measuring Student Development

The success of any student-oriented MIS depends heavily on the relevance of student outcome data to institutional objectives. While every institution needs to develop its own specific outcome measures, at least three types of measures are relevant to the educational objectives of most institutions. These "core" measures should be included in any student-oriented MIS:

1. *Successful completion of a program of study.* In its simplest form, this measure involves a dichotomy: the student either completes a degree or drops out. A more sophisticated approach is to determine whether a student's undergraduate achievements are consistent with that student's plans at college entry. For example, for the student who enters college planning to become a lawyer, simple completion of the undergraduate degree may not be a sufficient measure of success, given the stringent admissions requirements of law school. Thus, it might be more appropriate to use admission to law school as a criterion of successful completion. In other words, different criteria of success may be required for different students.

2. *Cognitive development.* Virtually all colleges and universities are concerned with their students' cognitive development. Most institutions, however, limit their assessment to the traditional grade-point average. Since grades reflect the student's relative level of performance at a particular point in time, they may not indicate accurately what the student has learned. Thus, meaningful evaluation of cognitive development probably requires some form of re-

peated measurement which assesses change by comparing the student's performance level at two or more points in time. If repeated measurement of cognitive functioning is for some reason found to be unfeasible, there are simple alternatives available. Research on learning, for example, suggests that study time may be a good surrogate measure of student learning.

3. *Student satisfaction.* The students' level of satisfaction with an institution's program is one of the most important indications of the program's effectiveness. One can measure overall satisfaction, but it is probably more useful to collect information on the students' degree of satisfaction with specific aspects of the college experience, such as the quality of teaching, advising, curriculum, facilities, extracurricular activities, and student services.

### Designing the Data Base

Student data are of three basic types: entry, process, and outcome. *Entry data* reflect the characteristics of students when they first enroll; *process data*, what happens to students while enrolled; and *outcome data*, the students' degree of attainment of desired educational or behavioral objectives. The distinction between process and outcome data is often imprecise. For example, a student's switching majors can be treated as a change in process, since the student is exposed to a different field of study, or as an outcome, since such a switch is usually a matter of the student's own choice. The distinction between process and outcome in this case is not intrinsic to the data; rather, it depends on how the data are used. Thus, if one is interested in how the student's major field affects some other outcomes (for example, the number of hours spent studying), the change in major can be regarded as a change in process. If one is interested in how the student's choice of a major is affected by some other process variable, then the change in field is treated as an outcome variable.

As was mentioned earlier, a student-oriented MIS should incorporate outcome data covering at least three areas: persistence, cognitive development, and satisfaction with the college experi-

ence. Student satisfaction is a useful category and a potentially rich
source of outcome data because it is relatively easy to assess and
it applies to many areas of the college experience. Students can
evaluate not only their academic programs and instruction but
also institutional services: orientation, registration, financial aid,
academic advisement, career counseling, personal counseling,
health services, job placement, and campus housing. They can
evaluate their residential facilities in terms of such characteristics as
privacy, roommate assignment, quiet for studying, food service,
and bathroom facilities. They can evaluate extracurricular activities, opportunities for independent study and social life, work
experience, contact with faculty members and student peers, and
so forth. Each institution must decide for itself which areas of satisfaction are most important.

## Critical Issues in Implementation

The first step in implementing a student-oriented MIS is to
determine what items of information are most needed in the preliminary system. For example, a modest beginning might entail a
simple survey that asks students to complete a diary showing how
they spend their time and to rate various aspects of the institutional
experience (the quality of classroom teaching, academic advising,
and so on). Ideally all segments of the academic community would
participate in designing the instrument, keeping it as short and as
simple as possible in this early stage.

The second step, the collection of data, should be planned to
occur at regular intervals (say, twice a year). Two important considerations here are sampling procedures and method of data collection. Since one should be able to create separate reports of results
at the departmental or school level, sampling should ensure that
each relevant organizational subunit is represented by an adequate
number of students. In large institutions, samples of respondents
could be rotated so that the same student is not surveyed more than
once a year. In smaller colleges, it might be necessary to sample the
same students more than once a year, particularly if separate

breakdowns of results by class year, sex, or other subgroupings are desired. Of the various possible survey methods (mail, personal interviews, and the like), perhaps the surest is to administer the survey during classes.

The dissemination of survey results is critical to the implementation process. As was mentioned above, in addition to institution-wide norms based on all respondents, there should be separate tabulations by department or school so that each subunit has a basis for evaluating its own data. Ideally, the institution should have access to comparative normative data from other institutions. The usefulness of such comparative norms in providing the institution with a broader perspective from which to view its own data more than compensates for any difficulties involved in establishing such interinstitutional consortium arrangements. Nor is it necessary for the institutions involved in such a cooperative venture to use identical survey instruments. (Such a requirement might well prove an insurmountable obstacle.) Perhaps the most that can be expected is that some of the survey items be common to all institutions.

Another consideration in dissemination is the administrative climate. If the administration intends to use the survey results as a basis for rewarding and punishing good and poor performance, then faculty and staff are likely to view all survey activity with hostility and suspicion. Moreover, such an attitude will encourage practitioners to manipulate the results. If, however, the administration sees its role as helping academic departments and administrative service units learn more about how they affect students, then personnel are more likely to view the survey as useful and constructive.

If institutions want to improve the education they offer their students, each individual instructor or administrator must evaluate his effectiveness and make appropriate changes. But it is very difficult for practicing professionals to confront their limitations and change established patterns. They must believe that the administration supports their attempts at self-evaluation and constructive change. While such an atmosphere of openness cannot be created overnight, the administration should strive to promote a positive and nonpunitive view of the student-oriented system.

The fourth implementation step is the interpretation of survey results and, where appropriate, the initiation of changes in policy or practice. This step is the most difficult and complex, as a hypothetical example will illustrate. Assume that students in the social sciences have rated the quality of academic advising as poor. Ideally, the social science departments would note this result, recognize it as a problem, and undertake appropriate remedial actions. In actuality, social science professors might well choose to interpret the low ratings in other ways, claiming that the evaluative questionnaire is phrased so as to bias the ratings by social science majors, that social science majors are by nature more critical of their professors, and so on. Such interpretations should not be dismissed as merely defensive. Rather, they should be regarded as testable propositions to be proved or refuted: by trying out a new rating item, or by producing other evidence of the more critical nature of social science majors. Such intellectual issues will be actively debated and fairly tested only when an atmosphere of openness and constructive self-improvement is encouraged and rewarded. In other words, when top administrators make difficult choices about departmental competition for limited resources, their final decisions should favor and reward openness and receptivity to constructive change.

The final step in the implementation process completes the MIS cycle: The student body is resurveyed to assess change in institutional effectiveness. This second survey not only provides an objective means for determining if remedial actions have been effective but also constitutes an "early warning system" for detecting unanticipated changes. The cyclical nature of the student-oriented information system satisfies two important needs: the assessment of changes in institutional functioning and the improvement of the student information system itself, as the results of each new survey suggest items to be changed, deleted, or added.

Student time, of course, is a major category of process and outcome information. Some institutions may be reluctant to collect time diaries from students on the grounds that the estimates will be crude and insensitive to changes in policy. A study of college environments several years ago indicates quite the contrary (Astin, 1968). Students attending a nationwide sample of 246 undergraduate institutions were asked how many hours per week, on the average, they spent in various activities. The variation among institutions is remarkable. These data clearly show that student bodies can differ widely in the time they devote to particular activities.

A hypothetical example will illustrate how student time diary information can be used in institutional evaluation and decision making. Assume that an institution has been collecting diary information for three student behaviors: sleeping, studying, and commuting. The information has been collected on a quarterly basis, and administrators now have data from the last two academic years and from the first two quarters of the current academic year. They note that the average amount of time that students spend sleeping has remained fairly stable at about fifty hours a week throughout the period. Hours spent studying have been relatively high during the fall and winter quarters and have declined during the spring quarter for the past two years. During the first two quarters of the current year, however, study hours have failed to show the increase observed in earlier years. This failure to replicate earlier trends suggests that other factors may have effected a reduction in the number of hours that students devote to studying. In other words, the failure to replicate trends from earlier years may be an early warning sign of potential problems. Hours spent commuting were extremely consistent during the first two years but increased during the current year.

Although the data do not provide a basis for drawing firm conclusions about the reasons for the decline in study hours, the administrators note the increase in commuting time and suggest a possible explanation: Students may be studying less because they are commuting more. These concomitant trends thus provide a basis for decision makers to develop and test alternative hypotheses to account for these trends. For example, it may be that changes in parking regulations introduced in the current year have increased the amount of commuting time. Alternatively, changes in admissions and recruitment policies may have increased the number of commuters. To test the association between commuting and study hours, administrators could cross-tabulate commuting and studying to see if students who commute more study less. Still other explanations are, of course, possible and can be tested because the needed data are available. Thus, the availability of time-series data allows decision makers to detect changes in critical student behavior and to test various explanations for such changes. In this way, changes in institutional policy or program can develop from analyses of actual student behavior.

## Possible Benefits

A fully operating student-oriented management information system has a number of advantages over more conventional administrative systems. One weakness of traditional attempts at institutional evaluation—including the typical case study prepared for accrediting teams—is that only a few people within the academic community are involved in developing the data base and interpreting results. A comprehensive student-oriented system, in comparison, could theoretically involve all members of the academic community—chief administrators as well as faculty and students—in the complex task of interpreting the data and devising appropriate policies.

A closely related virtue of the student-oriented approach is that the dialogue concerning institutional policy is diverted from a preoccupation with budgets and resources to a concern with the educational development of students. Discussions about funding are inherently competitive and conflict-ridden because if one group gets more money, other groups necessarily get less. If financial discussions focus on the educational development of students, however, then all interested parties share common objectives. The improvement of the educational effectiveness of any one unit does not limit or inhibit the ability of other units to do the same. Although a student-oriented system cannot obviate the need for budgetary debates, the decisions about budgetary allocations would be determined by their intended educational outcomes.

A student-oriented system could also provide economic benefits to institutions by favorably affecting their enrollments. A properly run student-oriented system could eventually help to reduce attrition rates. Further, a strongly student-oriented institution might eventually attract more applicants: The information network among prospective college students is such that the word eventually reaches students about what institutions have particularly interesting or special programs.

### Getting Started

A major shortcoming of institutional self-studies is that they are often done for the benefit of an accrediting team, rather than as a regular part of the institution's information-gathering activity. All too often, decision makers fail to see the need for *ongoing* self-analysis as an essential part of the management process.

How does an administration begin to modify its information-gathering and self-assessment activities in the ways suggested here? Administrators must first ask a few pointed questions. What kind of information concerning student involvement or lack of involvement is currently available to chief administrators? Do instructors and advisors regularly have access to data on students' academic involvement and academic progress? Do student personnel administrators periodically receive information on students' extracurricular activities and social life? Are appropriate data disseminated in comprehensible form and are such reports timely? Does the top administration take the initiative to survey faculty and staff needs for information on student progress and development? Is the administration responsive to requests for better information? What does the administration know about the quality of instruction as perceived by students in various departments? What do students think of the advising they receive in various departments? How adequate are different types of student services?

The mere asking of such questions is one means of making an administration more aware of the need for this type of information and of its potential value in planning and decision making. In a sense, the student-oriented system represents a continuing institutional evaluation. Too many administrators accept the idea that evaluation is something to do only when a particular problem needs to be resolved. Unfortunately, the nature of institutional politics is such that, once a problem has been identified and positions have been taken, no amount of objective data collection and self-study will budge people from their preconceived positions. In other words, a student-oriented management system designed primarily to provide data to solve institutional conflicts will probably not be very useful. However, the student-oriented system can be extremely useful in identifying problems before they have come to the attention of the academic community and before political positions have been taken.

## A Final Word

The view presented here—that institutions need to take a student-oriented approach to administration and planning—implies a concept of quality that deviates considerably from traditional definitions. Thus, under this new conception, a high-quality institution is one that knows about its students: how they are spending their time, how involved they are in the institution's academic and nonacademic activities, and how they judge the effectiveness of the institution's services. Further, the high-quality institution has a method for gathering and disseminating this information, enabling it to make appropriate adjustments in programs or policies when the student data indicate that change or improvement is needed. In other words, quality is equated here not with physical facilities or faculty credentials but rather with a continuing process of critical self-examination that focuses on the institution's contribution to the student's intellectual and personal development.

# APPENDIX A

# Chief Academic Officer's Personal Interview Questions

~~~~~~~~~~~~~~~~~~~~~~~~

Note to Interviewer: It is not necessary to ask all subquestions if respondent has already begun an answer. Just be sure that some response to subquestions has been provided. Be flexible and remember to budget your interview time.

*Interview Schedule for Academic Officers*

1. You mentioned in the questionnaire that you heard about the EXXON/RAMP project from _____. What has been your involvement in this project?

2. a. Do you expect any changes in the way your office is run as a result of your EXXON/RAMP grant?

   If yes: What will they be?

    b. What other changes, unrelated to RAMP, would you like to see occur in the operation of your department?

 3. Could you describe briefly for me the major features of your academic program?

    a. Have there been any major changes recently in the academic program of the college?

    b. What was (were) it (they)?

    c. What circumstances led to this change?

    d. Could you explain how the change was implemented? (*Probe: How did this come about? What was the background? What new information precipitated the change? What was the source?*)

    e. Whose decision was it to make the change? (*Probe: Whose support did you need to enlist?*)

    f. What obstacles were there? (*Probe: Were certain people against it? Who?*)

    g. What do you foresee as benefits of the change?

 4. a. What do you consider to be the most outstanding feature of your academic program?

    Why?

    b. What aspect of your academic program do you consider to be the weakest?

    Why?

      i. If you were to change this feature of the program, how would you do it?

      ii. Why have you not dropped it?

c. What is the present status of that situation?

d. In general, what kinds of information would you like that you do not currently have?

e. What information do you get now that seems superfluous or that you don't really need?

Now I would like to ask you a few questions about the role of your office in financial matters.

5. a. How is the budget for your office determined?

b. What is your role in the process?

c. Has your institution received any funds for improvements in the area of academic affairs? Identify the program, its goals, and source of funding.

Now we would like to hear some of your perceptions of what it is like to work in this academic environment.

6. How would you characterize your college president's style of operation?

7. How would you characterize your own administrative style?

8. What are the toughest decisions you have to make and what makes them so tough?

9. In making major decisions, do you have certain associates whose opinions you particularly value?

Who are they?

a. How often do you consult with them?

b. When and where does this usually take place?

   c. Are any of them unusual in terms of formal lines of authority (for example, informal contacts with persons either at
   your institution or outside your institution)?

10. Considering all of the forces you have to contend with in your
everyday activities, what obstacles do you encounter in performing your job?

How do you cope with them?

11. Knowing what you know now, what would you do differently
during your tenure as an academic officer?

Our questions have touched on many different areas. Is there any
aspect of the college or of your job which you would like to elabo-
rate on?

Would you take a few extra minutes to complete this questionnaire? [The interviewer gives the interviewee the questionnaire reproduced in Appendix B.] I can either wait until you complete it,
or you can return it to me in this preaddressed envelope.
If you have any second thoughts or additional things you would
like us to know, or questions you would like to ask, here is our
address.

Please feel free to contact us.
Thank you very much for your cooperation.

# APPENDIX B

# *Sample Questionnaire for Chief Academic Officer*

~~~~~~~~~~~~~~~~~~~~~~~~~~~~~~~~~~~~~

Dear Colleague:

The Exxon Education Foundation has asked us to undertake a program of research in connection with its Resource Allocation Management Program (RAMP). As you may know, a major purpose of RAMP is to encourage the effective use of modern management techniques in private institutions. Exxon will eventually award RAMP grants to 60 private, four-year colleges during the next three years.

Since your institution was recently selected as a RAMP grant recipient, our research team is currently making plans to visit your campus to interview key members of the administration. Our study will address two somewhat different issues: How will the implementation of the RAMP project affect the recipient institution? and How will each institution's general style and approach to management affect the quality of the college experience for students? We plan to assess each institution before and after management changes are implemented (with appropriate design modifications in the event your institution is well on the way to completing its RAMP project) and also to compare recipient institutions with those that did not receive RAMP grants. We expect the results of this study to provide college administrators with an improved body of data and theory on which to base their future administrative endeavors and revisions of management techniques.

The attached questionnaire will familiarize you with the areas we will be discussing during our interview with you the week of _____. We would appreciate your completing this questionnaire before our research team arrives on campus so we may follow up on relevant items during our discussion. Your individual responses to questions will be entirely confidential.

Thank you for your cooperation.

Higher Education Research Institute

1.  **Age:**_____

2.  **Sex:**

    Male . . . . . . . . . . . . . . . . . . . . . . . . . . 1
    Female . . . . . . . . . . . . . . . . . . . . . . . . 2

3.  **Field:**_____

4.  **Highest degree attained:**

    Bachelors . . . . . . . . . . . . . . . . . . . . . . . 1
    Masters . . . . . . . . . . . . . . . . . . . . . . . . 2
    Doctorate . . . . . . . . . . . . . . . . . . . . . . . 3
    Other postgraduate or professional . . . . . . . . . . . . . 4

5.  **How long have you been at this institution?**_____

6.  **Have you...** (Circle one response for each item.)

    |                                                          | Yes | No |
    |----------------------------------------------------------|-----|----|
    | Taught any undergraduate courses in the last three years? | 1   | 2  |
    | Taken a statistics or research methods course?           | 1   | 2  |
    | Had experience working with computers?                    | 1   | 2  |

7.  **How many dependents do you have?**_____

8.  **Do you have other sources of income, totaling more than $5,000?**

    Yes . . . . . . . . . . . . . . . . . . . . . . . . . . 1
    No . . . . . . . . . . . . . . . . . . . . . . . . . . . 2

9a. **When did you first hear about the RAMP project?**

    _____
    Approximate Date

    **From whom?**_____
    Name and Position

9b. **That was:** (Circle one.)

    Prior to the proposal . . . . . . . . . . . . . . . . . . . 1
    During the proposal study . . . . . . . . . . . . . . . . . 2
    At time of decision to apply . . . . . . . . . . . . . . . . 3
    After application . . . . . . . . . . . . . . . . . . . . . 4
    At time of award . . . . . . . . . . . . . . . . . . . . . 5
    At time of implementation . . . . . . . . . . . . . . . . . 6
    Other (Specify):_____ . . . . . . . . . 7

10. From the list below, please select what you consider
your institution's three strongest qualities and three
weakest qualities (those most in need of improvement
or strengthening).

| | Strongest Qualities (Circle 3) | Most in Need of Improvement or Strengthening (Circle 3) |
|---|---|---|
| Overall institutional reputation . . . . . | 1 | 1 |
| Financial soundness . . . . . . . . . | 2 | 2 |
| Goodwill of contributors. . . . . . . . | 3 | 3 |
| Alumni support . . . . . . . . . . . | 4 | 4 |
| Scholarly accomplishment of faculty (research) . . . . . . . . . . . | 5 | 5 |
| Faculty participation in governance . . . | 6 | 6 |
| Faculty morale . . . . . . . . . . . | 7 | 7 |
| Quality of teaching . . . . . . . . . . | 8 | 8 |
| Academic freedom . . . . . . . . . . | 9 | 9 |
| Scope of curricular programs . . . . . . | 10 | 10 |
| Academic ability of students . . . . . . | 11 | 11 |
| Institutional impact on student's academic development . . . . . . | 12 | 12 |
| Institutional impact on student's professional development. . . . . . | 13 | 13 |
| Institutional impact on student's personal or character development. . . . . | 14 | 14 |
| Community service programs . . . . . . | 15 | 15 |
| Good relations with community . . . . . | 16 | 16 |
| Other (Specify):_____ . . . | 17 | 17 |

**11a. Which three qualities do you think your president considers the strongest of the institution? Which three does he consider most in need of improvement or strengthening?**

| | Strongest Qualities (Circle 3) | Most in Need of Improvement or Strengthening (Circle 3) |
|---|---|---|
| Overall institutional reputation . . . . . | 1 | 1 |
| Financial soundness . . . . . . . . . | 2 | 2 |
| Goodwill of contributors. . . . . . . . | 3 | 3 |
| Alumni support . . . . . . . . . . . | 4 | 4 |
| Scholarly accomplishment of faculty (research) . . . . . . . . . . . | 5 | 5 |
| Faculty participation in governance . . . | 6 | 6 |
| Faculty morale . . . . . . . . . . . | 7 | 7 |
| Quality of teaching . . . . . . . . . . | 8 | 8 |
| Academic freedom . . . . . . . . . . | 9 | 9 |
| Scope of curricular programs . . . . . . | 10 | 10 |
| Academic ability of students . . . . . . | 11 | 11 |
| Institutional impact on student's academic development . . . . . . | 12 | 12 |
| Institutional impact on student's professional development. . . . . . | 13 | 13 |
| Institutional impact on student's personal or character development. . . . . . | 14 | 14 |
| Community service programs . . . . . . | 15 | 15 |
| Good relations with community . . . . . | 16 | 16 |
| Other (Specify):_____ . . . | 17 | 17 |

**11b. How confident are you of your perception of the President's position?** (Circle one.)

Very confident . . . . . . . . . . . . . . . . . . . . . . . . . 3
Somewhat confident . . . . . . . . . . . . . . . . . . . . . . . 2
Not confident . . . . . . . . . . . . . . . . . . . . . . . . . 1

12. We would like to find out which facts about your institution you have in your head. WITHOUT CONSULTING ANY OUTSIDE SOURCES, please give your best estimate for each of the following items. Then if you are not sure your estimate is correct, please provide the actual figure (if available) and the source. (Please identify the document, name of person consulted, or other source.)

| | Your Initial Estimate | Actual Figure | Source of Actual Figure |
|---|---|---|---|
| Current full-time day student enrollment (Registrar's figure) . . | | | |
| Number of full-time freshmen enrolled this year . . . . . . . | | | |
| Number of full-time freshmen enrolled last year . . . . . . . | | | |
| Average SAT scores of this year's freshmen (Specify if ACT or other test) . . . . . . Math | | | |
| . . . . . . Verbal | | | |
| Proportion of freshmen completing their baccalaureate degrees in four years. . . . . . . . . | % | % | |
| Size of full-time faculty (FTE) . . . | | | |
| Customary teaching load of full-time faculty member . . . . | Credit hours | Credit hours | |
| Percentage of faculty members holding rank of lecturer or instructor . | % | % | |
| Percentage of faculty members holding rank of assistant professor . . . . . . . . . . | % | % | |
| Percentage of faculty members holding rank of associate professor . . . . . . . . . . | % | % | |
| Percentage of faculty members holding rank of full professor . . | % | % | |
| The two *least expensive* departments at your institution (measured in terms of budgetary allocations per student credit-hour including faculty salaries and fringe benefits) . . . . . . | | | |
| The two *most expensive* departments at your institution (measured in terms of budgetary allocations per student credit-hour including faculty salaries and fringe benefits) . . . . . . | | | |

13. **In performing the duties of your office, how frequently do you have *personal* contact (including telephone conversations) with the following persons or categories of persons?** (Circle one response for each person. Omit response for your own position if listed.)

| | Several Times Daily | About Once A Day | Several Times Each Week | About Once A Week | Monthly | Less Than Monthly |
|---|---|---|---|---|---|---|
| Chief executive officer . . . | 6 | 5 | 4 | 3 | 2 | 1 |
| Staff of chief executive officer . | 6 | 5 | 4 | 3 | 2 | 1 |
| Other academic officers (deans, etc.) . . . . . | 6 | 5 | 4 | 3 | 2 | 1 |
| Chief fiscal or planning officer . | 6 | 5 | 4 | 3 | 2 | 1 |
| Chief student affairs officer . . | 6 | 5 | 4 | 3 | 2 | 1 |
| Chief admissions officer . . . | 6 | 5 | 4 | 3 | 2 | 1 |
| Financial aid officer . . . . | 6 | 5 | 4 | 3 | 2 | 1 |
| Registrar . . . . . . . . | 6 | 5 | 4 | 3 | 2 | 1 |
| Department chairpersons (Collectively) . . . . . | 6 | 5 | 4 | 3 | 2 | 1 |
| Other faculty . . . . . . . | 6 | 5 | 4 | 3 | 2 | 1 |
| Other administrative officers . | 6 | 5 | 4 | 3 | 2 | 1 |
| Students . . . . . . . . | 6 | 5 | 4 | 3 | 2 | 1 |
| Potential donors . . . . . . | 6 | 5 | 4 | 3 | 2 | 1 |
| Potential students . . . . . | 6 | 5 | 4 | 3 | 2 | 1 |
| Outside consultants . . . . | 6 | 5 | 4 | 3 | 2 | 1 |
| Visitors (other than above) . . | 6 | 5 | 4 | 3 | 2 | 1 |

**14.   How frequently do you use the means below to communicate with the following persons? F = frequently; O = occasionally; N = seldom or never.** (After each person circle one response for each method.)

| | Through Immediate Staff or Other Intermediaries | Letters or Memoranda | Personal Telephone Calls | Personal Conversations | Formal Group Meetings | Informal Meetings |
|---|---|---|---|---|---|---|
| Chief executive officer. | F O N | F O N | F O N | F O N | F O N | F O N |
| Chief fiscal officer . . | F O N | F O N | F O N | F O N | F O N | F O N |
| Chief student affairs officer . . . . . | F O N | F O N | F O N | F O N | F O N | F O N |
| Chief admissions officer . . . . . | F O N | F O N | F O N | F O N | F O N | F O N |
| Your immediate staff . | F O N | F O N | F O N | F O N | F O N | F O N |
| Departmental chairpersons (Collectively) . . | F O N | F O N | F O N | F O N | F O N | F O N |
| Other faculty . . . . | F O N | F O N | F O N | F O N | F O N | F O N |
| Students . . . . . . | F O N | F O N | F O N | F O N | F O N | F O N |

**15.   On the average during the academic year, what percent of your normal working time do you spend as follows?**

**Percent**

On campus . . . . . . . . . . . . . . . . . . .  _____
Off campus:
    Conducting institutional business . . . . . . . . . .  _____
    Attending meetings, conferences, etc. . . . . . . . .  _____
    Other (Specify):_____  . . . . . . . .  _____
        TOTAL  . . . . . . . . . . . . . . .       100

**16a. How do you value the following behaviors in your professional subordinates? VI = very important; SI = somewhat important; NI = not important; NEG = negative characteristic.** (Circle one response for each item.)

|                                              | VI | SI | NI | NEG |
|----------------------------------------------|----|----|----|-----|
| Initiative . ,                               | 4  | 3  | 2  | 1   |
| Creativity                                   | 4  | 3  | 2  | 1   |
| Scholarship                                  | 4  | 3  | 2  | 1   |
| Aggressiveness                               | 4  | 3  | 2  | 1   |
| Willingness to take risks                    | 4  | 3  | 2  | 1   |
| Interpersonal skills                         | 4  | 3  | 2  | 1   |
| Willingness to accept authority              | 4  | 3  | 2  | 1   |
| Influence with those in power                | 4  | 3  | 2  | 1   |
| Cooperation                                  | 4  | 3  | 2  | 1   |
| Support from faculty                         | 4  | 3  | 2  | 1   |
| Competitiveness                              | 4  | 3  | 2  | 1   |
| Professional or technical competence. .      | 4  | 3  | 2  | 1   |
| Willingness to "apple-polish".               | 4  | 3  | 2  | 1   |
| Effectiveness in dealing with students .     | 4  | 3  | 2  | 1   |
| Personal ambition                            | 4  | 3  | 2  | 1   |
| Salesmanship                                 | 4  | 3  | 2  | 1   |
| Frankness in dealing with others  . . . .    | 4  | 3  | 2  | 1   |
| Other (Specify):_____              | 4  | 3  | 2  | 1   |

**16b. In your judgment on what basis are administrators rewarded at your institution? VD = very descriptive; SD = somewhat descriptive; ND = not descriptive of behavior leading to reward.** (Circle one response for each item.)

|                                              | VD | SD | ND |
|----------------------------------------------|----|----|----|
| Initiative                                   | 3  | 2  | 1  |
| Creativity                                   | 3  | 2  | 1  |
| Scholarship                                  | 3  | 2  | 1  |
| Aggressiveness                               | 3  | 2  | 1  |
| Willingness to take risks                    | 3  | 2  | 1  |
| Interpersonal skills                         | 3  | 2  | 1  |
| Willingness to accept authority              | 3  | 2  | 1  |
| Nepotism or "buddyism"                       | 3  | 2  | 1  |
| Influence with those in power                | 3  | 2  | 1  |
| Cooperation                                  | 3  | 2  | 1  |
| Support from faculty                         | 3  | 2  | 1  |
| Competitiveness                              | 3  | 2  | 1  |
| Professional or technical competence.        | 3  | 2  | 1  |
| Willingness to "apple-polish".               | 3  | 2  | 1  |
| Effectiveness in dealing with students       | 3  | 2  | 1  |
| Personal ambition                            | 3  | 2  | 1  |
| Salesmanship                                 | 3  | 2  | 1  |
| Frankness in dealing with others             | 3  | 2  | 1  |
| Other (Specify):_____              | 3  | 2  | 1  |

17. **How satisfied are you with the following aspects of your job? VS = very satisfied; SS = somewhat satisfied; NS = not satisfied.** (Circle one response for each item.)

| | VS | SS | NS |
|---|---|---|---|
| Salary . . . . . . . . . . . . . . . . . | 3 | 2 | 1 |
| Fringe benefits . . . . . . . . . . . . | 3 | 2 | 1 |
| Status of my position . . . . . . . . . . | 3 | 2 | 1 |
| Status of this institution . . . . . . . . . | 3 | 2 | 1 |
| Autonomy in decision making . . . . . . . | 3 | 2 | 1 |
| Variety in activities . . . . . . . . . . . | 3 | 2 | 1 |
| Power . . . . . . . . . . . . . . . . . | 3 | 2 | 1 |
| Influence . . . . . . . . . . . . . . . | 3 | 2 | 1 |
| Congenial work relationships . . . . . . . . | 3 | 2 | 1 |
| Competency of colleagues . . . . . . . . . | 3 | 2 | 1 |
| Opportunities for different (better) jobs at this college . . . . . . . . . . . | 3 | 2 | 1 |
| Visibility for jobs at other institutions . . . . . | 3 | 2 | 1 |
| Challenge . . . . . . . . . . . . . . . | 3 | 2 | 1 |
| Responsibility . . . . . . . . . . . . . . | 3 | 2 | 1 |
| Relations with students . . . . . . . . . . | 3 | 2 | 1 |
| Job security . . . . . . . . . . . . . . | 3 | 2 | 1 |
| Opportunity for scholarly pursuits . . . . . . | 3 | 2 | 1 |
| Availability of time to spend with family . . . . | 3 | 2 | 1 |
| Opportunity for leisure time . . . . . . . . | 3 | 2 | 1 |
| Other (Specify): _____ | 3 | 2 | 1 |

18. **How often do you rely on the following sources to find out what goes on in other areas of the administration?** (Circle one response for each item.)

| | Frequently | Occasion- ally | Seldom or Never |
|---|---|---|---|
| Meetings . . . . . . . . . . | 3 | 2 | 1 |
| Personal conversations with people involved . . . . . . | 3 | 2 | 1 |
| Newsletter . . . . . . . . . | 3 | 2 | 1 |
| Memoranda . . . . . . . . . | 3 | 2 | 1 |
| Gossip, hearsay or through the grapevine . . . . . . . | 3 | 2 | 1 |
| Student newspaper . . . . . . | 3 | 2 | 1 |
| Local press . . . . . . . . | 3 | 2 | 1 |
| Speeches by relevant authorities . | 3 | 2 | 1 |
| Formal reports . . . . . . . . | 3 | 2 | 1 |
| Through the faculty . . . . . . | 3 | 2 | 1 |
| Other (Specify): _____ . | 3 | 2 | 1 |

**Thank you for your cooperation.**

# APPENDIX C

# *Sample Questionnaire for Faculty*

〰〰〰〰〰〰〰〰〰〰〰〰〰〰〰〰

Dear Colleague:

The Exxon Education Foundation has asked us to undertake a program of research in connection with its Resource Allocation Management Program (RAMP). As you may know, a major purpose of RAMP is to encourage the effective use of modern management techniques in private institutions. Exxon will award RAMP grants to 60 private, four-year colleges during the next three years.

We are interested in two somewhat different issues: How will implementation of RAMP programs affect the management of colleges? and What effect will changes in management have on the members of the academic community, faculty, students, and others? It is this latter issue we consider vital. Therefore, your experiences and perceptions are crucial to our study.

**177**

We appreciate the heavy demand on your time, but we hope you will take a few minutes to complete the following questionnaire and return it to us in the attached self-addressed envelope.

Thank you very much for your time and effort.

Higher Education Research Institute

1. **Age:**_____

2. **Sex:**
   Male . . . . . . . . . . . . . . . . . . . . . . . . . . . . . 1
   Female . . . . . . . . . . . . . . . . . . . . . . . . . . . 2

3. **Field:**_____

4. **Highest degree attained:**
   Bachelors . . . . . . . . . . . . . . . . . . . . . . . . . . 1
   Masters . . . . . . . . . . . . . . . . . . . . . . . . . . . 2
   Doctorate . . . . . . . . . . . . . . . . . . . . . . . . . . 3
   Other postgraduate or professional . . . . . . . . . . . . . 4

5. **How long have you been at this institution?**_____

6. **Have you . . .** (Circle one response for each item.)

   |                                                              | Yes | No |
   |--------------------------------------------------------------|-----|----|
   | Done administrative work in the last three years             | 1   | 2  |
   | Taken a statistics or research methods course                | 1   | 2  |
   | Had experience working with computers.                       | 1   | 2  |

7. **How many dependents do you have?**_____

8. **Do you have other sources of income, totaling more than $5,000?**
   Yes . . . . . . . . . . . . . . . . . . . . . . . . . . . . . 1
   No . . . . . . . . . . . . . . . . . . . . . . . . . . . . . . 2

9. We would like to find out which facts about your institution you have in your head. WITHOUT CONSULTING
ANY OUTSIDE SOURCES, please give your best estimate
for each of the following items. Then if you are not sure
your estimate is correct, please provide the actual figure
(if available) and the source. (Please identify the documen t,
name of person consulted, or other source.)

| | Your Initial Estimate | Actual Figure | Source of Actual Figure |
|---|---|---|---|
| Current full-time day student enrollment (Registrar's figure) . . | _____ | _____ | _____ |
| Number of full-time freshmen enrolled this year . . . . . . . | _____ | _____ | _____ |
| Number of full-time freshmen enrolled last year . . . . . . . | _____ | _____ | _____ |
| Average SAT scores of this year's freshmen (Specify if ACT or other test) . . . . . Math | _____ | _____ | _____ |
| . . . . . Verbal | _____ | _____ | _____ |
| Proportion of freshmen completing their baccalaureate degrees in four years . . . . . . . . | _____% | _____% | _____ |
| Size of full-time faculty (FTE) . . . | _____ | _____ | _____ |
| Average salary paid this academic year by your institution for assistant professor . . . . . . | $_____ | $_____ | _____ |
| Average salary for associate professor | $_____ | $_____ | _____ |
| Average salary for full professor . . . | $_____ | $_____ | _____ |

10a. What do you consider the most outstanding feature of
your institution's academic program?

_____

Why?_____

10b. What aspect of your institution's academic program do
you consider the weakest?

_____

Why?_____

**11.** **From the list below, please select what you consider your institution's three strongest qualities and three weakest qualities (those most in need of improvement or strengthening).**

|  | Strongest Qualities (Circle 3) | Most in Need of Improvement or Strengthening (Circle 3) |
|---|---|---|
| Overall institutional reputation . . . . . | 1 | 1 |
| Financial soundness . . . . . . . . . | 2 | 2 |
| Goodwill of contributors. . . . . . . . | 3 | 3 |
| Alumni support . . . . . . . . . . . | 4 | 4 |
| Scholarly accomplishment of faculty (research) . . . . . . . . . . . | 5 | 5 |
| Faculty participation in governance . . . | 6 | 6 |
| Faculty morale . . . . . . . . . . . | 7 | 7 |
| Quality of teaching . . . . . . . . . . | 8 | 8 |
| Academic freedom . . . . . . . . . . | 9 | 9 |
| Scope of curricular programs . . . . . . | 10 | 10 |
| Academic ability of students . . . . . . | 11 | 11 |
| Institutional impact on student's academic development . . . . . . | 12 | 12 |
| Institutional impact on student's professional development. . . . . . | 13 | 13 |
| Institutional impact on student's personal or character development. . . . . . | 14 | 14 |
| Community service programs . . . . . . | 15 | 15 |
| Good relations with community . . . . . | 16 | 16 |
| Other (Specify):_____ . . . | 17 | 17 |

**We would also like some specifics about your role as a faculty member at your college.**

**12.** **What percent of your working time each year do you spend in each of the following activities?**

|  | Per Cent |
|---|---|
| Teaching . . . . . . . . . . . . . . . . . . . . . . . | _____ |
| Research-scholarship . . . . . . . . . . . . . . . . . . | _____ |
| Professional activities . . . . . . . . . . . . . . . . . | _____ |
| Committees Specify:_____. . . . . . . . . . | _____ |
| _____. . . . . . . . . . | _____ |
| _____. . . . . . . . . . | _____ |
| Administrative tasks (other than committees) . . . . . . . | _____ |
| TOTAL . . . . . . . . . . . . . . . . . . . | 100 |

13.  **In your role as a faculty member, how frequently do you have *personal* contact (incuding telephone conversations) with the following persons or categories of persons?** (Circle one response for each person.)

| | Several Times Daily | About Once A Day | Several Times Each Week | About Once A Week | Monthly | Less Than Monthly |
|---|---|---|---|---|---|---|
| Chief executive officer . . . | 6 | 5 | 4 | 3 | 2 | 1 |
| Staff of chief executive officer. | 6 | 5 | 4 | 3 | 2 | 1 |
| Chief academic officer . . . | 6 | 5 | 4 | 3 | 2 | 1 |
| Other academic officers (deans, etc.) . . . . . | 6 | 5 | 4 | 3 | 2 | 1 |
| Chief fiscal or planning officer. | 6 | 5 | 4 | 3 | 2 | 1 |
| Chief student affairs officer. . | 6 | 5 | 4 | 3 | 2 | 1 |
| Chief admissions officer . . . | 6 | 5 | 4 | 3 | 2 | 1 |
| Financial aid officer . . . . | 6 | 5 | 4 | 3 | 2 | 1 |
| Registrar . . . . . . . . . | 6 | 5 | 4 | 3 | 2 | 1 |
| Your department chairperson . . . . . . | 6 | 5 | 4 | 3 | 2 | 1 |
| Other faculty . . . . . . . | 6 | 5 | 4 | 3 | 2 | 1 |
| Other administrative officers . | 6 | 5 | 4 | 3 | 2 | 1 |
| Students . . . . . . . . . | 6 | 5 | 4 | 3 | 2 | 1 |
| Potential donors . . . . . . | 6 | 5 | 4 | 3 | 2 | 1 |
| Potential students . . . . . | 6 | 5 | 4 | 3 | 2 | 1 |
| Outside consultants . . . . | 6 | 5 | 4 | 3 | 2 | 1 |
| Visitors (other than above) . . | 6 | 5 | 4 | 3 | 2 | 1 |

14. How frequently do you use the means below to communicate with the following persons? **F = frequently;
O = occasionally; N = seldom or never.** (After each person
circle one response for each method.)

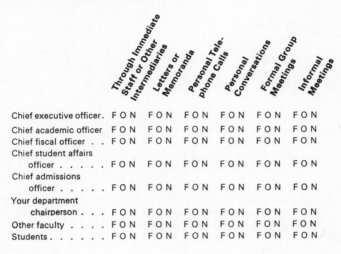

|  | Through Immediate Staff or Other Intermediaries | Letters or Memoranda | Personal Tele-phone Calls | Personal Conversations | Formal Group Meetings | Informal Meetings |
|---|---|---|---|---|---|---|
| Chief executive officer. | F O N | F O N | F O N | F O N | F O N | F O N |
| Chief academic officer | F O N | F O N | F O N | F O N | F O N | F O N |
| Chief fiscal officer . . | F O N | F O N | F O N | F O N | F O N | F O N |
| Chief student affairs officer . . . . . | F O N | F O N | F O N | F O N | F O N | F O N |
| Chief admissions officer . . . . . | F O N | F O N | F O N | F O N | F O N | F O N |
| Your department chairperson . . . | F O N | F O N | F O N | F O N | F O N | F O N |
| Other faculty . . . . | F O N | F O N | F O N | F O N | F O N | F O N |
| Students . . . . . . | F O N | F O N | F O N | F O N | F O N | F O N |

15a. **How often do you rely on the following sources *to find
out* what goes on in the administration of your college?**
(Circle one response for each item.)

|  | Frequently | Occasion-ally | Seldom or Never |
|---|---|---|---|
| Meetings . . . . . . . . . | 3 | 2 | 1 |
| Personal conversations with people involved . . . . . . | 3 | 2 | 1 |
| Newsletter . . . . . . . . | 3 | 2- | 1 |
| Memoranda . . . . . . . . | 3 | 2 | 1 |
| Gossip, hearsay or through the grapevine . . . . . . . | 3 | 2 | 1 |
| Student newspaper . . . . . . | 3 | 2 | 1 |
| Local press . . . . . . . . | 3 | 2 | 1 |
| Speeches by relevant authorities . | 3 | 2 | 1 |
| Formal reports . . . . . . . | 3 | 2 | 1 |
| Through the faculty . . . . . | 3 | 2 | 1 |
| Other (Specify):_____ | 3 | 2 | 1 |

**15b. How often do you rely on the following sources *to provide input* to the administration?** (Circle one response for each item.)

|  | Frequently | Occasion-<br>ally | Seldom<br>or Never |
|---|---|---|---|
| Meetings . . . . . . . . . . | 3 | 2 | 1 |
| Personal conversations with<br>   people involved . . . . . . | 3 | 2 | 1 |
| Newsletter . . . . . . . . . | 3 | 2 | 1 |
| Memoranda . . . . . . . . . | 3 | 2 | 1 |
| Gossip, hearsay or through<br>   the grapevine . . . . . . . | 3 | 2 | 1 |
| Student newspaper . . . . . . | 3 | 2 | 1 |
| Local press . . . . . . . . | 3 | 2 | 1 |
| Speeches by relevant authorities . | 3 | 2 | 1 |
| Formal reports . . . . . . . | 3 | 2 | 1 |
| Through the faculty . . . . . . | 3 | 2 | 1 |
| Other (Specify):_____ | 3 | 2 | 1 |

**16a. Can you give an example of some important information in the academic realm of administration which has recently come to your attention?**

_____

_____

**16b. How did you hear about it?** (Circle one.)

Meetings . . . . . . . . . . . . . . . . . . . . . . . . . . 1
Personal conversations with people involved . . . . . . . . . . . 2
Newsletter . . . . . . . . . . . . . . . . . . . . . . . . . 3
Memoranda . . . . . . . . . . . . . . . . . . . . . . . . 4
Gossip, hearsay or through the grapevine . . . . . . . . . . . . 5
Student newspaper . . . . . . . . . . . . . . . . . . . . . . 6
Local press . . . . . . . . . . . . . . . . . . . . . . . . 7
Speeches by relevant authorities . . . . . . . . . . . . . . . . 8
Formal reports . . . . . . . . . . . . . . . . . . . . . . . 9
Through the faculty . . . . . . . . . . . . . . . . . . . . .10
Other (Specify):_____ . . . . . . . . . .11

**16c. Who is responsible for informing you about such matters?** (Circle one.)

Faculty in my department . . . . . . . . . . . . . . . . . . . 1
Faculty in other departments . . . . . . . . . . . . . . . . . . 2
Chairperson of my department . . . . . . . . . . . . . . . . . 3
Chairpersons of other departments . . . . . . . . . . . . . . . 4
Students . . . . . . . . . . . . . . . . . . . . . . . . . . 5
Administrators . . . . . . . . . . . . . . . . . . . . . . . . 6
Other (Specify):_____ . . . . . . . . . . . 7

**17. Who is responsible for informing you about salary adjustments?** (Circle one.)

Other faculty in my department . . . . . . . . . . . . . . . . . 1
Chairperson of my department . . . . . . . . . . . . . . . . 2
Administrators . . . . . . . . . . . . . . . . . . . . . . . . 3
Other (Specify):_____ . . . . . . . . . . 4

**18. Do you normally receive student enrollment lists for each course you teach?** (Circle one.)

YES . . . . . . . . . . . . . . . . . . . . . . . . . . . . . . 1
NO . . . . . . . . . . . . . . . . . . . . . . . . . . . . . . . 2

**19a. If you have research funds or other extramural monies do you personally maintain records of your budget?** (Circle one.)

YES . . . . . . . . . . . . . . . . . . . . . . . . . . . . . . 1
NO . . . . . . . . . . . . . . . . . . . . . . . . . . . . . . . 2
No research funds . . . . . . . . . . . . . . . . . . . . . . . 3

**19b. Does any other person (office) maintain records of your budget?** (Circle one.)

YES . . . . . . . . . . . . . . . . . . . . . . . . . . . . . . 1
NO . . . . . . . . . . . . . . . . . . . . . . . . . . . . . . . 2

**20. How satisfactory are support services in the following areas?** (Circle one response for each item.) **VS = very satisfactory; SS = somewhat satisfactory; NS = not satisfactory.**

|  | VS | SS | NS |
|---|---|---|---|
| Typing . . . . . . . . . . . . . . . | 3 | 2 | 1 |
| Budgeting . . . . . . . . . . . . . . | 3 | 2 | 1 |
| Research assistance . . . . . . . . . . | 3 | 2 | 1 |
| Administrative assistance . . . . . . . . | 3 | 2 | 1 |
| Other (Specify):_____ . . . . . | 3 | 2 | 1 |

**21. Considering all the forces you encounter in your everyday activities, what obstacles do you face in performing your job? How do you cope with them?**

_____

_____

_____

22. **How would you characterize your college president's style of operation?**

_____

_____

_____

23. **In your judgment on what basis are administrators rewarded at your institution? VD = very descriptive; SD = somewhat descriptive; ND = not descriptive of behavior leading to reward.** (Circle one response for each item.)

|  | VD | SD | ND |
|---|---|---|---|
| Initiative | 3 | 2 | 1 |
| Creativity | 3 | 2 | 1 |
| Scholarship | 3 | 2 | 1 |
| Aggressiveness | 3 | 2 | 1 |
| Willingness to take risks | 3 | 2 | 1 |
| Interpersonal skills | 3 | 2 | 1 |
| Willingness to accept authority | 3 | 2 | 1 |
| Nepotism or "buddyism" | 3 | 2 | 1 |
| Influence with those in power | 3 | 2 | 1 |
| Cooperation | 3 | 2 | 1 |
| Support from faculty | 3 | 2 | 1 |
| Competitiveness | 3 | 2 | 1 |
| Professional or technical competence | 3 | 2 | 1 |
| Willingness to "apple-polish" | 3 | 2 | 1 |
| Effectiveness in dealing with students | 3 | 2 | 1 |
| Personal ambition | 3 | 2 | 1 |
| Salesmanship | 3 | 2 | 1 |
| Frankness in dealing with others | 3 | 2 | 1 |
| Other (Specify):_____ | 3 | 2 | 1 |

**24.** **How satisfied are you with the following aspects of your job? VS = very satisfied; SS = somewhat satisfied; NS = not satisfied.** (Circle one response for each item.)

|  | VS | SS | NS |
|---|---|---|---|
| Salary . . . . . . . . . . . . . . . . . | 3 | 2 | 1 |
| Fringe benefits . . . . . . . . . . . . | 3 | 2 | 1 |
| Status of my position . . . . . . . . . . | 3 | 2 | 1 |
| Status of this institution . . . . . . . . | 3 | 2 | 1 |
| Autonomy in decision making . . . . . . | 3 | 2 | 1 |
| Variety in activities . . . . . . . . . . . | 3 | 2 | 1 |
| Power . . . . . . . . . . . . . . . . . | 3 | 2 | 1 |
| Influence . . . . . . . . . . . . . . | 3 | 2 | 1 |
| Congenial work relationships . . . . . . | 3 | 2 | 1 |
| Competency of colleagues . . . . . . . . | 3 | 2 | 1 |
| Opportunities for different (better) jobs at this college . . . . . . . . . . . | 3 | 2 | 1 |
| Visibility for jobs at other institutions . . . . . | 3 | 2 | 1 |
| Challenge . . . . . . . . . . . . . . | 3 | 2 | 1 |
| Responsibility . . . . . . . . . . . . . | 3 | 2 | 1 |
| Relations with students . . . . . . . . . | 3 | 2 | 1 |
| Job security . . . . . . . . . . . . . | 3 | 2 | 1 |
| Opportunity for scholarly pursuits . . . . . . | 3 | 2 | 1 |
| Availability of time to spend with family . . . . | 3 | 2 | 1 |
| Opportunity for leisure time . . . . . . . . | 3 | 2 | 1 |
| Other (Specify):_____ | 3 | 2 | 1 |

**Thank you for your cooperation.**

# APPENDIX D

# *Sample Questionnaire for Students*

~~~~~~~~~~~~~~~~~~~~~~~~~~~~~~~~~~~~~~~~~~~~~

Dear Student:

Your college is one of a number of institutions that has been awarded a grant from the Exxon Education Foundation to assist in the improvement of administrative practices and procedures in private colleges.

Our organization, the Higher Education Research Institute, has been asked to do a study of the effects of these grants and of other changes in the administration of private colleges. We want to find out what effect changes have on the different members of the academic community— administrators, faculty, and students. Your input is crucial to our study.

Please take a few minutes to complete the following questionnaire and return it to the front of the class when you're through. Please *do not* put your name on the questionnaire. We want all respondents to remain anonymous.

Thank you for your assistance.

Higher Education Research Institute

**1. What is your sex?** (Circle one.)

Male . . . . . . . . . . . . . . . . . . . . . . . . . 1
Female . . . . . . . . . . . . . . . . . . . . . . . . 2

**2. What is your college class?** (Circle one.)

Freshman . . . . . . . . . . . . . . . . . . . . . . . 1
Sophomore . . . . . . . . . . . . . . . . . . . . . . . 2
Junior . . . . . . . . . . . . . . . . . . . . . . . . 3
Senior . . . . . . . . . . . . . . . . . . . . . . . . 4
Graduate . . . . . . . . . . . . . . . . . . . . . . . 5
Other (Specify):_____. . . . . . . . . . . 6

**3. Where are you presently living? If you had a choice, where would you prefer to live?** (Circle one response in each column.)

| | Live Now | Prefer to Live |
|---|---|---|
| With parents or relatives | 1 | 1 |
| Other private home, apartment or room | 2 | 2 |
| College dormitory | 3 | 3 |
| Fraternity or sorority | 4 | 4 |
| Other campus student housing | 5 | 5 |
| Other (Specify):_____ | 6 | 6 |

**4. How much education do each of your parents have?** (Circle one response for each parent.)

| | Father | Mother |
|---|---|---|
| Elementary school | 1 | 1 |
| Some high school | 2 | 2 |
| High school degree | 3 | 3 |
| Some college | 4 | 4 |
| College degree | 5 | 5 |
| Some graduate school | 6 | 6 |
| Graduate or professional degree | 7 | 7 |

5. **What is your involvement in the following student organizations?** (Circle one response for each organization.)

| | Presently a Member | Not a Member but Interested | Not Interested |
|---|---|---|---|
| Fraternity or sorority . . . . . . . | 3 | 2 | 1 |
| Student religious groups. . . . . . | 3 | 2 | 1 |
| Subject-matter clubs (e.g., French Club, Political Science Club) . . . . . . . . | 3 | 2 | 1 |
| Student government committees . . | 3 | 2 | 1 |
| Student newspaper staff. . . . . . | 3 | 2 | 1 |
| Literary magazine staff . . . . . . | 3 | 2 | 1 |
| Freshman handbook staff . . . . . | 3 | 2 | 1 |
| Radio station staff . . . . . . . . | 3 | 2 | 1 |
| Student yearbook staff . . . . . . | 3 | 2 | 1 |
| Choir . . . . . . . . . . . . . | 3 | 2 | 1 |
| Band or orchestra . . . . . . . . | 3 | 2 | 1 |
| Theatre group . . . . . . . . . . | 3 | 2 | 1 |
| Other (Specify):_____ . . . | 3 | 2 | 1 |

6. **How often have you used the following student services?** (Circle one response for each item.)

| | Frequently | Sometimes | Never |
|---|---|---|---|
| Transcript distribution. . . . . . . . . . | 3 | 2 | 1 |
| Financial aid advice . . . . . . . . . . | 3 | 2 | 1 |
| Curriculum advisement . . . . . . . . . | 3 | 2 | 1 |
| Career counseling . . . . . . . . . . . | 3 | 2 | 1 |
| Personal counseling . . . . . . . . . . | 3 | 2 | 1 |
| Health services . . . . . . . . . . . . | 3 | 2 | 1 |
| Employment placement . . . . . . . . . | 3 | 2 | 1 |
| On-campus housing . . . . . . . . . . | 3 | 2 | 1 |
| Other (Specify):_____ . . . . . | 3 | 2 | 1 |

7. **How satisfactory are the following services or procedures at your school? VS = very satisfactory; SS = somewhat satisfactory; NS = not satisfactory; NA = not applicable or not familiar with it.** (Circle one response for each item.)

| | VS | SS | NS | NA |
|---|---|---|---|---|
| Orientation | 3 | 2 | 1 | 0 |
| Registration | 3 | 2 | 1 | 0 |
| Distribution of grade reports | 3 | 2 | 1 | 0 |
| Distribution of transcripts | 3 | 2 | 1 | 0 |
| Financial aid | 3 | 2 | 1 | 0 |
| Curriculum advisement | 3 | 2 | 1 | 0 |
| Career counseling | 3 | 2 | 1 | 0 |
| Personal counseling | 3 | 2 | 1 | 0 |
| Health services | 3 | 2 | 1 | 0 |
| Employment placement | 3 | 2 | 1 | 0 |
| On-campus housing | 3 | 2 | 1 | 0 |
| Other (Specify):_____ | 3 | 2 | 1 | 0 |

8. **To what extent are the following values important to you in your education? VI = very important; SI = somewhat important; NI = not important.** (Circle one response for each item.)

| | VI | SI | NI |
|---|---|---|---|
| Academic growth | 3 | 2 | 1 |
| Vocational preparation | 3 | 2 | 1 |
| Developing interest in music and art | 3 | 2 | 1 |
| Independent thinking and behavior | 3 | 2 | 1 |
| Interaction with people of different backgrounds | 3 | 2 | 1 |
| Prestigious degree | 3 | 2 | 1 |
| Having a good time in college | 3 | 2 | 1 |
| Preparation for professional training | 3 | 2 | 1 |
| Intellectual growth and appreciation of ideas | 3 | 2 | 1 |
| Developing a satisfying philosophy of life | 3 | 2 | 1 |
| Developing a direction for career or life's work | 3 | 2 | 1 |
| Developing the confidence to take a stand on things I believe in | 3 | 2 | 1 |
| Other (Specify):_____ | 3 | 2 | 1 |

9. **How would you characterize your political views?** (Circle one.)

Far left . . . . . . 1
Liberal . . . . . . 2
Middle of the road . . . . . . 3
Conservative . . . . . . 4
Far right . . . . . . 5

10. How descriptive of you are each of the following? VD = very descriptive; SD = somewhat descriptive; ND = not descriptive. (Circle one response for each item.)

|  | VD | SD | ND |
|---|---|---|---|
| Self-confident. | 3 | 2 | 1 |
| Independent | 3 | 2 | 1 |
| Friendly | 3 | 2 | 1 |
| Can stick to a job | 3 | 2 | 1 |
| Self-controlled | 3 | 2 | 1 |
| Intellectually curious | 3 | 2 | 1 |
| Have specific academic goals. | 3 | 2 | 1 |
| Good leadership. | 3 | 2 | 1 |
| Other (Specify):_____ | 3 | 2 | 1 |

11. How much have you valued each of the following during the past year? (Circle one response for each item.)

|  | Great Deal | Moder- ately | Not at All |
|---|---|---|---|
| Course work in my major field | 3 | 2 | 1 |
| Extracurricular organizational activities | 3 | 2 | 1 |
| Individual or independent research or study | 3 | 2 | 1 |
| Social life (dating, parties, etc.) | 3 | 2 | 1 |
| Course work in general | 3 | 2 | 1 |
| Friendships. | 3 | 2 | 1 |
| Job experience | 3 | 2 | 1 |
| Contacts with faculty member(s) | 3 | 2 | 1 |
| Other (Specify):_____ | 3 | 2 | 1 |

12. To what extent does the display of the following behaviors help people get good grades in your institution? (Circle one response for each item.)

|  | Great Deal | Moder- ately | Not at All |
|---|---|---|---|
| Initiative. | 3 | 2 | 1 |
| Creativity | 3 | 2 | 1 |
| Scholarship. | 3 | 2 | 1 |
| Aggressiveness | 3 | 2 | 1 |
| Interpersonal skills | 3 | 2 | 1 |
| Deference | 3 | 2 | 1 |
| Cooperation | 3 | 2 | 1 |
| Competitiveness. | 3 | 2 | 1 |
| Competence | 3 | 2 | 1 |
| "Apple-polishing" | 3 | 2 | 1 |
| Salesmanship. | 3 | 2 | 1 |
| Other (Specify):_____ | 3 | 2 | 1 |

13a. On approximately what date did you register for classes this term?

Month / Day / Year

\_\_\_\_\_ / \_\_\_ / \_\_\_

13b. How long did it take you to register?

_____Hours or fraction thereof

13c. In how many of your first-choice classes were you able to enroll?

_____ of _____

13d. Is registration computerized at your college? (Circle one.)

YES     NO

If YES, on approximately what date(s) did you receive your computer-verified class list?

Month / Day / Year

\_\_\_\_\_ / \_\_\_ / \_\_\_

13e. Describe briefly the procedure for changing your class schedule after registration._____

_____

_____

13f. Was classroom space adequate for all your classes? (Circle one.)

YES     NO

13g. Were laboratory facilities adequate? (Circle one.)

YES     NO

**14.** **Did you apply for financial aid for this academic year?**
(Circle one.)

      YES      NO

**If YES, please answer the following questions.**

|  | Month / Day / Year |
|---|---|
| On approximately what date did you apply? | _____ / ____ / ___ |

What forms were required? (Please list.)

_____

_____

_____

On approximately what date did you receive notification of the results
of your application?

      Month / Day / Year

      _____ / ____ / ___

Did you talk with a financial aid counselor at this college? (Circle one.)

      YES      NO

If YES, please answer the following: (Circle one response for each item.)

Did he/she have your file or data quickly

| at his/her disposal? . . . . . . . . . . . YES | NO |
|---|---|
| Was it accurate? . . . . . . . . . . . . . YES | NO |
| Was it complete? . . . . . . . . . . . . YES | NO |

**15.** **Which of the following sources of financing enable you**
**to attend college?** (Circle all that apply.)

| Part-time job . . . . . . . . . . . . . . . . . . . . . . . . . . . . . | 1 |
|---|---|
| Parental support . . . . . . . . . . . . . . . . . . . . . . . . . . . | 2 |
| Own savings . . . . . . . . . . . . . . . . . . . . . . . . . . . . . | 3 |
| Scholarship or grant . . . . . . . . . . . . . . . . . . . . . . . . . | 4 |
| Loan . . . . . . . . . . . . . . . . . . . . . . . . . . . . . . . . . | 5 |
| Work-study . . . . . . . . . . . . . . . . . . . . . . . . . . . . . . | 6 |
| Other (Specify): _____ . . . . . . . . . . . | 7 |

16. **Did you apply for dormitory or campus student housing?**
(Circle one.)

    YES　　NO

**If YES, please answer the following questions.**

Month / Day / Year

On approximately what date did you apply?　　___ / ___ / ___

On approximately what date did you receive notification of the results of your application?

Month / Day / Year

___ / ___ / ___

If you are living in a dormitory or other campus student housing, please answer the following:

How many roommates do you have? (Circle one.)

0　　1　　2　　more

Did you choose your roommate(s)? (Circle one.)

YES　　NO

Were there any complications in your housing when you arrived on campus? (Circle one.)

YES　　NO

If YES, please explain briefly:

_____

_____

_____

**How adequate is your college residence with respect to the following? VA = very adequate; SA = somewhat adequate; NA = not adequate.**
(Circle one response for each item.)

| | VA | SA | NA |
|---|---|---|---|
| Privacy | 3 | 2 | 1 |
| Quiet for studying | 3 | 2 | 1 |
| Lounges or sitting areas | 3 | 2 | 1 |
| Room size | 3 | 2 | 1 |
| Bathroom facilities | 3 | 2 | 1 |
| Heat | 3 | 2 | 1 |
| Student freedom | 3 | 2 | 1 |
| Programming (Lectures, films, etc.) | 3 | 2 | 1 |

What are the major strong points of your residence hall?

_____

_____

_____

What are the major deficiencies of your residence hall?

_____

_____

_____

17a. Is the faculty at your institution concerned about and interested in the needs of students? (Circle one.)

A great deal . . . . . . . . . . . . . . . . . . . . . . . . . . . . . 3
Moderately . . . . . . . . . . . . . . . . . . . . . . . . . . . . . 2
Not at all . . . . . . . . . . . . . . . . . . . . . . . . . . . . . 1

17b. During the past year, how many different faculty members did you seek out to discuss your course work progress or related questions? (Circle one.)

Not at college past year . . . . . . . . . . . . . . . . . . . . . . 1
None . . . . . . . . . . . . . . . . . . . . . . . . . . . . . . . 2
One . . . . . . . . . . . . . . . . . . . . . . . . . . . . . . . 3
Two . . . . . . . . . . . . . . . . . . . . . . . . . . . . . . . 4
Three . . . . . . . . . . . . . . . . . . . . . . . . . . . . . . 5
Four . . . . . . . . . . . . . . . . . . . . . . . . . . . . . . . 6
Five . . . . . . . . . . . . . . . . . . . . . . . . . . . . . . . 7
Six or more . . . . . . . . . . . . . . . . . . . . . . . . . . . 8

17c. During the past year with how many instructors or teachers did you become *well* acquainted? (Circle one.)

Not at college past year . . . . . . . . . . . . . . . . . . . . . . 1
None . . . . . . . . . . . . . . . . . . . . . . . . . . . . . . . 2
One . . . . . . . . . . . . . . . . . . . . . . . . . . . . . . . 3
Two . . . . . . . . . . . . . . . . . . . . . . . . . . . . . . . 4
Three . . . . . . . . . . . . . . . . . . . . . . . . . . . . . . 5
Four . . . . . . . . . . . . . . . . . . . . . . . . . . . . . . . 6
Five . . . . . . . . . . . . . . . . . . . . . . . . . . . . . . . 7
Six or more . . . . . . . . . . . . . . . . . . . . . . . . . . . 8

18a. Is the administration of your institution concerned about and interested in the needs of students? (Circle one.)

A great deal . . . . . . . . . . . . . . . . . . . . . . . . . . . . 3
Moderately . . . . . . . . . . . . . . . . . . . . . . . . . . . . 2
Not at all . . . . . . . . . . . . . . . . . . . . . . . . . . . . . 1

**18b. During the past year how many different administrators did you seek out?** (Circle one.)

Not at college past year . . . . . . . . . . . . . . . . . . . . . . . 1
None . . . . . . . . . . . . . . . . . . . . . . . . . . . . . . . 2
One . . . . . . . . . . . . . . . . . . . . . . . . . . . . . . . 3
Two . . . . . . . . . . . . . . . . . . . . . . . . . . . . . . . 4
Three . . . . . . . . . . . . . . . . . . . . . . . . . . . . . . 5
Four . . . . . . . . . . . . . . . . . . . . . . . . . . . . . . . 6
Five . . . . . . . . . . . . . . . . . . . . . . . . . . . . . . . 7
Six or more . . . . . . . . . . . . . . . . . . . . . . . . . . . 8

**18c. During the past year with how many administrators did you become *well* acquainted?** (Circle one.)

Not at college past year . . . . . . . . . . . . . . . . . . . . . . . 1
None . . . . . . . . . . . . . . . . . . . . . . . . . . . . . . . 2
One . . . . . . . . . . . . . . . . . . . . . . . . . . . . . . . 3
Two . . . . . . . . . . . . . . . . . . . . . . . . . . . . . . . 4
Three . . . . . . . . . . . . . . . . . . . . . . . . . . . . . . 5
Four . . . . . . . . . . . . . . . . . . . . . . . . . . . . . . . 6
Five . . . . . . . . . . . . . . . . . . . . . . . . . . . . . . . 7
Six or more . . . . . . . . . . . . . . . . . . . . . . . . . . . 8

**19. Prior to your enrollment, how quickly did the information (catalog, application, financial aid) you requested from the college arrive?** (Circle one.)

> **Very Quickly**    5    4    3    2    1    **Very Slowly**

**On approximately what date did you apply for admission to this college?**

> Month / Day / Year
>
> _____ / ___ / ___

**Was your acceptance from this college a personal or form letter?** (Circle one.)

> Personal Letter . . . . . . 1      Form Letter . . . . . . . . 2

**Was your acceptance letter from this college the first, middle or last acceptance you received from the schools to which you applied?** (Circle one.)

> First . . . . . . 1    Middle . . . . . 2    Last . . . . . . 3

20. **Do you agree or disagree with the items below?** (Circle one response for each item.)

|                                                                                    | Strongly Agree |   |   |   | Strongly Disagree |
|------------------------------------------------------------------------------------|:---:|:---:|:---:|:---:|:---:|
| You were very confident about what to expect upon arriving at your institution . . . . . . . . . . . | 5 | 4 | 3 | 2 | 1 |
| Your expectations of the institution were the same as the reality you experienced when you arrived . . . | 5 | 4 | 3 | 2 | 1 |

21. **The institution conducted an on-campus orientation for freshmen.** (Circle one.)

    Yes . . . . . . 1    No . . . . . . 2    Don't Know . . . 3

    **Did you attend the orientation?** (Circle one.)

    Yes . . . . . . 1    No . . . . . . 2

    **How long did the orientation last?**

    _____

    **How useful was the information given at the orientation?** (Circle one.)

    **Very Useful**    5    4    3    2    1    **Not Useful**

22. **How difficult did you find each of the following in your adjustment to college? VD = very difficult; SD = somewhat difficult; ND = not difficult.** (Circle one response for each item.)

|                                                          | VD | SD | ND |
|----------------------------------------------------------|:---:|:---:|:---:|
| Getting to know faculty members . . . . .                | 3 | 2 | 1 |
| Being away from home and friends . . . .                 | 3 | 2 | 1 |
| Earning satisfactory grades . . . . . . . .              | 3 | 2 | 1 |
| Meeting and knowing other students of both sexes . . . . . . . . . . . | 3 | 2 | 1 |
| Living within budget . . . . . . . . . .                 | 3 | 2 | 1 |
| Managing time . . . . . . . . . . . . .                  | 3 | 2 | 1 |
| Studying efficiently. . . . . . . . . . .                | 3 | 2 | 1 |
| Selecting a major field of study and/or a career . . . . . . . . . . . . . | 3 | 2 | 1 |
| Other (Specify):_____ . . . . .                  | 3 | 2 | 1 |

**Thank you for your cooperation.**

# APPENDIX E

# Coding Scheme
# for Faculty Responses

Here is a coding scheme for faculty responses to the question: "How would you characterize your college president's style of operation?"

| Code | Sample Responses |
|---|---|
| Open | open, straightforward, friendly, supportive, personal, accessible, listens, accepts input |
| Democratic | delegates, decentralized, democratic |
| Efficient | efficient, well-organized, businesslike, fiscally minded, makes tough decisions |
| Remote | devious, no information, doesn't express opinions, political, remote, not consultative, far from campus operation, bureaucratic |

| Code | Sample Responses |
| --- | --- |
| Authoritarian | does what he wants, autocratic, authoritarian |
| Ineffective | erratic, ineffective |
| Entrepreneurial | fund raiser, public relations expert, entrepreneur, operator |
| Intellectual | knowledgeable about higher education, academically inspiring, intelligent |
| Nonacademic | not academically inspiring, not a scholar |

# APPENDIX F

# *Detailed Profiles of Chief Administrators*

~~~~~~~~~~~~~~~~~~~~~~~~~~~~~~~~

In this appendix, we draw upon data from both the questionnaire and the interviews to give a more detailed picture of each type of administrator: the qualities they value in subordinates, their job satisfaction, their patterns of communication, their views about the toughest decisions they have to make and the major sources of their frustration, their comments about what they would do differently if they had that option, and (in the case of middle managers) the adequacy of their input into the decision-making process. Separate summaries are presented for academic officers, fiscal officers, development officers, student affairs officers, registrars, admissions officers, and financial aid officers.

## Academic Officers

Of the forty-five academic officers who completed questionnaires, thirty-nine are men. This group of administrators averages
forty-five years of age and has been at the institution a mean of ten
years. As mentioned in Chapter Two, they are more likely than any
other group of administrators to hold the doctorate (91 percent)
and to have taught undergraduates within the three years prior to
the survey (65 percent).

The traits they most value in their professional subordinates
are initiative, interpersonal skills, professional or technical competence, and cooperation. A larger proportion of academic officers
than of other groups of administrators (including presidents) also
say that they value scholarship and faculty support as attributes of
their subordinates, and a smaller proportion are concerned that
their subordinates have influence with those in power. These values seem to reflect a more scholarly or academic orientation than
that of any other group of administrators.

Academic officers seem generally more satisfied with their
jobs than do other administrators, with the exception of presidents.
Curiously, they are even more likely than presidents to express
high satisfaction with their influence. The specific aspects of the
job that they are most likely to find satisfying are responsibility,
variety in activities, challenge, and status of the position. A larger
proportion of academic officers than of any other group (except
presidents) mention personal status as a source of satisfaction—not
surprising, since they occupy the number two position at their institutions. They are also more satisfied than are other administrators with their power and influence, a finding consistent with their
central position in the communication network. Only about two in
five are optimistic about their chances for advancement within their
own institutions, and only 46 percent with their visibility for jobs at
other colleges, but these figures are nonetheless higher than that
for most other administrators.

Academic officers are more likely than other groups of administrators, however, to be dissatisfied with the status of the in-

stitution (consistent with the finding reported earlier that they are the only group who frequently cite institutional reputation as in need of strengthening) and with their relations with students. Perhaps, since they tend to come from the professorial ranks and to have experience teaching, they are more inclined than other administrators to feel that their current position isolates them from the mainstream of campus life and to miss having frequent contact with students.

Even so, academic officers are likely to say that they have personal contact with students almost daily. Others with whom they have relatively frequent contact are other academic officers, the president and his staff, faculty, the fiscal officer, the registrar, the student affairs officer, and other administrators. In contrast, they have contact no more than once a month, on the average, with potential donors, potential students, and outside consultants. The sources that they rely upon most frequently for information about other areas of administration are personal conversations with the people involved (98 percent report using this mode frequently) and meetings (70 percent indicate frequent use, and 30 percent occasional use, of this mode). In addition, they are somewhat more likely than other groups of administrators to rely frequently on formal reports, but less likely than others to cite frequent use of newsletters, the student newspaper, the local press, or speeches as a means of keeping themselves informed.

When asked in the interviews "Do you have certain associates whose opinions you particularly value?" the academic officers most often mention faculty, both individuals and groups such as faculty committees (cited by fourteen of the forty-eight academic officers interviewed). They value the opinions of faculty far more than do the presidents. This preference probably reflects not only their professorial backgrounds but also the necessities of their position. Other valued associates are deans (including associate and assistant deans), the president, and other administrators at the vice-presidential level.

Of the people outside the formal lines of authority whose opinions are sought by academic officers, faculty members again

are mentioned most frequently (by ten of the forty-eight interviewees). That more do not mention faculty in response to this
question is probably attributable to their perception of faculty as
within the college's formal lines of authority. Other groups mentioned in response to the question are off-campus groups, campus
middle managers, and students.

By far the toughest decisions academic officers make are
those that involve faculty hiring, firing, promotion, and tenure
(mentioned by thirty-nine of the forty-eight interviewees). Following are some typical comments: "Tenure decisions [are most
difficult], because people are dislocated personally and profession-
ally, and it's a small community"; and "My greatest difficulty came
last year when I had to cut five faculty while maintaining some degree of morale in this institution."

Decisions about financial matters take a distant second place
after personnel decisions, mentioned by six academic officers as
particularly tough. Finally, five academic officers mention lack of
information or data on which to base sound judgments.

Even though academic officers frequently turn to the faculty
for advice, and even though they tend to value faculty opinion,
they nonetheless often find the faculty frustrating to work with.
Eighteen of the interviewees mention faculty as sources of frustration, compared with seven who mention particular administrators,
and only three who mention students. Some typical responses to
the question "Who or what inhibits or frustrates you within your
institution?" are: "a small group of faculty whom I call the anti-
everything group," and "faculty arrogance and dishonesty." As is
true with the presidents, the tone that academic officers use in talking about the faculty is often exceptionally bitter:

- I wish the faculty were less doctrinaire and more realistic. . . . I
  wish they didn't buy myths about themselves: that faculty know
  best, that faculty have the ability to see the solutions to things
  without doing any homework. . . . I waste a lot of time keeping
  the faculty happy.

• The labor union is most frustrating to have to deal with. Some there have other agendas: they want to take over management of the institution; they would like to get rid of the administration. If they can't do that, they'd just as soon bring the institution down. They believe the state would take over. They're very wrong. They're naive in some ways, destructive in others.

Some academic officers respond to the question about the sources of frustration by mentioning specific problem areas rather than people. For instance, eight mention general administrative problems, and seven mention their institution's financial problems.

Finally, asked in the interviews what they would do differently if they could do things over again, the academic officers most frequently mention their handling of administrative matters (mentioned by seventeen) and their handling of faculty matters (mentioned by seven). Ten say that there is nothing they would do differently.

In summary, the academic officers in our study are clearly more involved with the faculty than with any other group. Indeed, their professional activities seem to revolve around the faculty, whose opinions are more highly valued than those of other associates; whose hiring, promotion, tenure, and firing constitute their most difficult decisions; and who are the chief cause of their frustration.

## Fiscal Officers

Fiscal officers are the oldest group of administrators (except presidents). The mean age of the thirty-two fiscal officers who completed questionnaires is forty-nine years, and all are men. Only 13 percent have the doctorate, and only 19 percent have taught undergraduates within the three years prior to the survey. About one in four report making more than $5,000 a year in outside income.

Of the qualities valued in subordinates, fiscal officers are most likely to mention initiative, cooperation, and professional or technical competence. In addition, two thirds—more than any other group except presidents—put a high premium on willingness to accept authority. On the other hand, fiscal officers are less likely than most groups of administrators to cite interpersonal skills, creativity, aggressiveness, competitiveness, and frankness as desirable traits for subordinates to have. The picture that emerges is one of a rather conservative, low-key group of men.

Like presidents and academic officers (though to a somewhat lesser degree), fiscal officers tend to be very satisfied with such extrinsic job features as personal status, power, fringe benefits, and salary, as well as with many of the intrinsic rewards of their jobs such as challenge, responsibility, and variety in activities. Interestingly, close to two in three (a higher proportion than of any other group of administrators) also express satisfaction with the status of the institution. Why their view on this matter should be so much more positive than that of the academic officer is not clear.

Although a majority (63 percent) mention congenial work relationships as a source of satisfaction, this proportion is lower than that for other administrators. They also evidence some dissatisfaction with opportunities for advancement in their own institutions and with visibility for jobs at other institutions. As with academic officers, the reason they hold this opinion may be simply that they already occupy very high positions. Moreover, because they lack the doctorate and the academic background, their chances of being advanced to college presidencies are rather remote.

With respect to personal contacts, fiscal officers seem somewhat more isolated than other groups of administrators. Their most frequent contacts (from several times a week to daily) are with their immediate staff, the president (though they see him less often than do the academic and development officers), the academic officer, and other administrators. They see the financial aid officer about once a week but are less likely than other groups of administrators to deal often with the admissions officer, the registrar, faculty, or students. Like academic officers, they are much more inclined than presidents to cite personal conversations as the means they use to keep informed about what is happening in the administration; close to three fourths say that they rely frequently on meetings for that purpose, and about two in five cite frequent use of memoranda. Newsletters, the student newspaper, the local press, and formal reports are likely to be an occasional rather than frequent source of information. None of the fiscal officers say that they depend frequently on gossip to keep informed (though two in five mention this as an occasional source), and none depend frequently on faculty (though three in five say that faculty occasionally are the source of information about other areas of the administration).

Interviews with forty-one fiscal officers yielded more detailed information about their communication patterns. The associates whose opinions they value most are the president, followed by vice-presidential officers and middle managers. A few mention deans and their own staff, but none mention faculty. (In contrast, academic officers name faculty members and deans as their most valued associates, with presidents ranking third.) Perhaps many college presidents concern themselves more with financial matters than with academic affairs and thus are seen as better sources of advice by fiscal officers than by academic officers.

Outside the formal lines of authority, fiscal officers are most likely to go to campus middle managers for advice (mentioned by eleven). Personal friends are also high on the list, as are business officers at other colleges (each rating five mentions). Five fiscal officers say they call upon bankers for advice, and another five name outside consultants. What is most striking here is, first, that once again faculty are not mentioned at all (though both presidents and chief academic officers cite them more frequently than any other group) and second, that fiscal officers rely far more than do presidents or academic officers on people who have no official connection with the college. Given the nature of their jobs, it is not surprising that they should go to business officers, bankers, and outside consultants for advice, but it is remarkable that several say they consult personal friends. In a sense, fiscal officers seem to be the most cosmopolitan, the least parochial, of the top administrative officers at liberal arts colleges.

Like academic officers, fiscal officers most frequently cite personnel decisions (especially firings) as the toughest decisions they have to make. Twenty-seven of the forty-one interviewed mention this area, and their comments make it clear that such decisions are very difficult for them: "It's tough to lay off lower-income people who need all the money they can get: for example, the fifty-year-old with no skills"; and "[The toughest decisions involve] recommendations related to the termination of individuals. I really care for people and hate to see them go through that kind of trauma."

One might think that financial decisions would be the toughest that fiscal officers have to make, since they are, after all, the administrators most responsible for the institution's financial affairs. But that area of concern ranks second, mentioned by twenty fiscal officers. Moreover, such decisions cause them much less anguish than do personnel decisions, as the dispassionate tone of the following comments indicates: "How to invest funds, how to manage an endowment"; "Any decision which has fiscal implications, for it involves explaining to well-meaning persons that they cannot get what they want"; and "[how to handle] situations where cost-benefit differences are unclear."

In addition, six fiscal officers mention decisions about the financial problems of students as being among the toughest they have to make; the chief issue they have to face is whether to dismiss students. On this issue, administrators' comments resemble their comments about having to fire employees: "It's a decision that affects the life of a person: for instance, if a student doesn't pay his bills, we have to suspend him"; and "[The toughest decision is whether] to accept or reject a student on the basis of his financial condition. If a student owes too much money, can he continue?"

Besides decisions involving personnel, institutional finances, and student finances, fiscal officers report various other challenging decisions that they have to make:

• A foreign student wasn't adjusting to his second year. It's bad for the school to lose a student. It has a bad impact on [other] students. He needs help but I don't know if we can help him.

• I have taken positions contrary to the Board of Trustees on some financial matters, which at times is risky. . . . It would have been easier to back down, but I didn't. Such decisions are always tough to make.
• [The toughest decisions involve] outside people who want something from the college. They contact me and ask that certain things be done. I can't comply with many requests but don't want to offend people with an interest in the college.

The chief sources of frustration among fiscal officers are personnel problems (mentioned by twenty-one of the forty-one interviewees), general administrative problems (mentioned by twenty), and financial problems (mentioned by nineteen). Six also cite such physical problems as lack of space and inadequate facilities. Since fiscal affairs officers are directly concerned with college finances, one might expect that financial problems would head the list of frustrations; but, as is the case with presidents and academic officers (who cite personnel problems involving faculty), personnel problems are more troublesome. The implication is that personnel problems are a leading cause of administrative frustrations at small colleges, even among fiscal officers, whose employees do not have tenure.

In response to the question "What would you do differently if you had it to do over again," the overwhelming majority (thirty-five of the forty-one fiscal officers interviewed) respond that they would handle certain administrative matters differently:

• [I would] establish a closer working relationship with the board of trustees.
• I would insist as a condition of employment in this environment that the treasurer be involved in the faculty committees or [be] a member of the faculty.
• I'd expect more from the people working for me and with me. I'd use closer supervision. I've found that independence isn't always a good philosophy.

Moreover, seven fiscal officers (compared with only three academic officers) say that they would get more formal training, or a different kind of formal training: "I would study more accounting"; and "I would get a legitimate ticket in the academic community—a master's, at least." Several reasons for their discontent in this area suggest themselves. First, as was pointed out earlier, fiscal officers probably have little chance of advancing to institutional presidencies because they lack the credentials and the academic background. Moreover, fiscal officers at small liberal arts colleges, comparing their responsibilities and salaries with those of fiscal officers in business and industry, probably do not feel that they have done as well as could be expected, whereas academic officers—most of whom probably started their careers aspiring to be full professors —may well feel that they have done as well or better than could be expected. Finally, fiscal officers may find it more difficult to keep up with the demands of their jobs, since they may require more specialized courses and materials than their colleges have to offer.

Seven fiscal officers say there is nothing they would do differently; three say they would arrange to have a larger staff; and three say that they would not have taken the job in the first place: "Knowing what I know now, I probably would not have taken the job. I left my last job for reasons of professional development, and I'm not sure I will get that here. This job will be a lot of accounting and record keeping."

In summary, even though fiscal officers are second only to college presidents in finding their jobs challenging, and even though—in contrast to most of their administrative colleagues— they do not come into conflict with faculty, they are not an untroubled group. They worry about having to fire employees (especially those who might have difficulty finding other jobs), they often face severe financial constraints, and they tend to feel that their positions are something of a dead end in that they lack the educational background to advance further. Finally, they seem to be less integrated into college life than most other types of administrators, as is indicated by their reliance on off-campus advisors.

### Development Officers

Of the thirty-two development officers who completed questionnaires, 90 percent are male, only 16 percent have the doctorate, and only 20 percent have taught undergraduates within the three years prior to the survey. Their mean age is forty-seven years. Close to three in ten (a larger proportion than any other group except presidents) earn more than $5,000 a year in outside income.

Cooperation, initiative, and professional or technical competence are the qualities they most value in their subordinates. Indeed, 100 percent indicate the first of these traits is very important. At the same time, they are more likely than are most other groups of administrators to give high priority to salesmanship (55 percent), aggressiveness (48 percent), personal ambition (39 percent), and competitiveness (29 percent) and less likely than others to value scholarship (10 percent), interpersonal skills (73 percent), and effectiveness in dealing with students (26 percent). This pattern of valued traits is distinctive among top administrators, suggesting that the duties of development officers lead them to take a more extroverted and aggressive approach to their jobs.

Development officers are generally less satisfied with their jobs than are presidents or academic and fiscal officers. Four in five say that they are satisfied with the challenge, variety, and responsibility that their jobs have to offer. But they are markedly less satisfied than are the administrators already discussed with the status of their positions, their power, and their salaries. This last point is interesting, since development officers are paid about as much as fiscal officers ("Administrators' Salaries . . . ," 1979), yet 55 percent of the latter group say they are very satisfied with their salaries, compared with only 39 percent of the development officers.

Like the other vice-presidents, development officers do not rate opportunities for advancement within their own institutions very highly, nor do they express great satisfaction with their visibility for jobs at other campuses. Only 35 percent are very satisfied with the status of their institutions; in this respect, they resemble academic officers. This somewhat jaundiced view may be attributable to the nature of their jobs: Since they compete with other colleges for funds, development officers may be more aware than most other administrators of the standing of their institutions in relation to others, at least in the eyes of potential benefactors and granting agencies. In addition, only 30 percent of the development officers express satisfaction about their relations with students (again, they resemble the academic officers on this point). This low rating may also be attributable to the nature of their jobs (development officers probably have less to do with students than any group of top administrators) rather than to any real dissatisfaction.

With respect to communication patterns, development officers seem to have many contacts with diverse individuals and groups. They report seeing potential donors daily or even several times a day (the only administrators who have such frequent contact with this group). Others with whom they have contact at least several times a week are their own staff, the president, other administrators, and the fiscal officers. They are also more likely than anyone but the president to see visitors frequently. However, they have less frequent contact with students than do most other groups.

As is true of academic and fiscal officers, the means which they most frequently use to keep informed about other areas of administration are personal conversations and meetings. About two in five rely frequently on memoranda, and about three in ten rely frequently on newsletter and formal reports. None report frequently relying on speeches (although 55 percent do so occasionally), and only 6 percent frequently consult the student newspaper for such information. Only one in five say they frequently rely on gossip, hearsay, or the grapevine, though 45 percent occasionally use such sources.

The associates whose opinions are most relied upon by development officers are other vice-presidential administrators (mentioned by nine interviewees), the president (mentioned by seven), outside consultants and middle managers (five mentions each), and trustees (mentioned by three). No officer mentions faculty or students. Comparing their responses to these questions with those of other administrators, we find that development officers are the only ones who report valuing the opinions of trustees, and the only ones besides fiscal officers who report valuing the opinions of outside consultants. They are, on the whole, less likely than other administrators to name the president of their institution.

In short, development officers seem even more isolated from campus life and the academic community than fiscal officers, who at least report valuing the opinions of deans. This impression is strengthened when we consider the people outside the formal lines of authority whom the development officers consult: they are most likely to consult trustees (mentioned by ten of the interviewees) or middle managers (six mentions). Although some say they frequently turn for advice to faculty members and to members of their own staff, they are—like fiscal officers—also inclined to seek advice from individuals or groups outside the institution: development officers at other colleges or at charitable institutions, outside consultants, their spouses, and personal friends.

Like academic and fiscal officers, development officers feel that their toughest decisions involve personnel matters, especially firings (mentioned by twenty-two of thirty-five development officers who were interviewed), general administrative problems (mentioned by eleven), and financial matters (mentioned by eight). One might expect that financial matters would rank highest among this group of administrators, since their main function is to raise money. Perhaps for this very reason, they are more inclined to view managing financial matters as a normal part of their jobs rather than as a particular problem. Those who do cite financial matters as constituting their toughest decisions sometimes mention difficulties with raising money: "[My problems] involve how to approach people, and one has to guess, subjectively, if one is approaching them properly for money"; and "I have been trying to decide what type of activities would be of best benefit to the college, to draw potential donors. If I blow it, it's bad." Almost as often, however, development officers mention problems involved in spending or allocating money: whether to continue underwriting a costly program or how to allocate scarce resources. Sometimes the responsibilities of development officers take them far afield from financial matters. One individual at a conservative church-affiliated college in the Midwest describes his toughest decision: "Do we carry in our alumni magazine announcements about alumni who have decided they are no longer closet homosexuals?"

The greatest sources of frustration for development officers are the general process of academic governance, personnel problems (not including faculty), and general administrative problems, with each mentioned by about one third of the interviewees. A few also mention problems in raising money and problems involving faculty, but none mention problems with students. Development officers are more inclined than any other group of administrators to feel frustrated by the process of academic governance itself, perhaps because they tend to come from business backgrounds and to maintain ties with the business world; thus, they may be more especially inclined to feel impatient with the slow pace of academic governance. Whatever the explanation, their distaste is clearly manifested in their comments:

• [I am most frustrated by] the natural sophistry of academic organizations, . . . the difficulty in getting a decision made.
• [There is a] lack of responsiveness from peers; [it takes time] to get something done after the decision is made.
• I can't identify any individual. The entire system frustrates me.
• The president and vice-president for administration [do not approach] problems from the management theory viewpoint. In the college's present state, we cannot afford to do this very long. Tactical versus strategic function of college misallocates resources.

As to what they would do differently if they were starting their careers over again, thirteen of the thirty-five development officers interviewed say they would handle administrative matters (other than those having to do with fund raising) differently, eight say they would handle fund raising differently, two say they would get more formal training, two say they would not have taken the job in the first place, and two say they would handle relations with faculty differently. Other responses reveal their business orientation: For instance, five say they would arrange to have a larger or a more competent staff, and two say they would have switched jobs more frequently during their careers to enhance their marketability. Finally, eleven claim very emphatically that they would do nothing differently.

In summary, even though development officers tend to be somewhat remote from the day-to-day life of the campus, having little involvement with students or with faculty members, even though they tend to be dissatisfied with some aspects of their jobs, and even though they are likely to be irritated by the process of academic governance, they nonetheless are inclined to believe that they have carried out their responsibilities and they seem generally confident of their success.

### Student Affairs Officers

The last group of vice-presidential administrators that we will consider are the student affairs officers. Of the thirty-nine who completed questionnaires, eight are women. Student affairs officers tend to be younger than other vice-presidential officers, with a mean age of forty-two years. They are more likely than any other group except academic officers to hold a doctorate (27 percent) and to have taught undergraduates within the three years prior to the survey (47 percent).

Initiative, effectiveness in dealing with students, interpersonal skills, cooperation, creativity, and professional or technical competence are the qualities that student affairs officers most value in their subordinates; indeed, they are more inclined to give high ratings to initiative and creativity than are other administrators. They are also singular in placing a high premium on risk taking. Among the traits that they are less likely than other administrators to value are personal ambition, salesmanship, competitiveness, and influence with those in power. The impression conveyed here is just the opposite of that for development officers: warmth, cooperativeness, and congeniality seem to characterize the student affairs officer's mode of operation.

Nonetheless, these administrators are less satisfied with many aspects of their jobs than are other vice-presidents. Only in the areas of challenge, variety, and responsibility do more than 70 percent express great satisfaction. About two thirds (a larger proportion than for any other group of top administrators) are also highly satisfied with their relations with students and with the congeniality of their work relationships. They are, however, less satisfied than are other vice-presidents with their personal status, power, and influence, and with the challenge and responsibility of their positions. There are several probable causes of this discontent. First, student affairs officers are mainly concerned with students, a lower-status group than the constituencies of the other vice-presidents. Second, because of the nature of their jobs, they are more campus-bound than are other top administrators; they have fewer opportunities to travel. Finally, as is revealed by their communication patterns (see the next paragraph), they have less prestige and power than the other vice-presidents, even though their positions are usually shown as equal on formal organization charts.

Student affairs officers have their most frequent contacts with students (typically, several times a day), followed by faculty and their own staff (from several times a day to daily), and the academic officer. They have relatively little contact with the president or the fiscal officer. As is true of other vice-presidents, their principal means of keeping informed about other areas of the administration are personal conversations and meetings. They are more likely than are other administrators (except for the president) to get such information from the faculty, much more likely than all other top-level administrators to rely on the student newspaper, but less likely to rely heavily on formal reports. About one in ten say that gossip is a frequent source of information, and 57 percent cite it as an occasional source.

The nature of the student affairs officers' job is further revealed by their responses to the question "Do you have certain associates whose opinions you particularly value?" Faculty are mentioned most frequently, followed by deans, the two groups who are most likely to have useful information about students. Some name the president as an associate whose opinion they value, but very few mention vice-presidents, probably because the latter group is too far removed from the students to be able to offer opinions valuable to the student affairs officer.

Faculty also head the list of people outside the formal lines of authority whose opinions are sought by student affairs officers (mentioned by twenty-two of the forty-eight interviewed). Students are the next most common outside authorities among student affairs officers, named by thirteen; it is somewhat disconcerting, however, that even at small private liberal arts colleges—institutions generally regarded as highly concerned with student development—only one fourth of the student affairs officers rely on the opinions of students. Others mentioned in this connection are deans, middle managers, and their own staff. In addition, when naming people to whom they turn for advice student affairs officers mention groups no other administrators cite: five mention townspeople, five mention local ministers or pastors, and three mention on-campus chaplains or ministers. This tendency to seek advice from clergy probably reflects the nature of their jobs; that is, their concern with the personal problems of students. Finally, three student affairs officers say they seek the opinion of their spouses, and three mention friends as a source of advice.

Consistent with their strong orientation toward and concern with students, a majority of student affairs officers report that their toughest decisions involve students. The following comments are typical:

- Whether to kick a kid out of school is always hard for me. Because of my counseling background, I always look for the ramifications of what that action might do.
- Taking kids out for psychological reasons [is difficult] because I always think they're salvageable. I'm torn by them because they're poignant, and they're usually brighter than most kids.
- [The toughest] are decisions about putting students on probation, dismissing students. The responsibility is enormous.
- Disciplining students [is difficult for me]. I dread it.

In addition, about two in five of the student affairs officers interviewed cite personnel decisions as being very difficult. (They concur with the other vice-presidential officers in this respect.)

Given their deep involvement with students, it is interesting that when student affairs officers are asked to indicate who or what frustrates or inhibits them most, not one mentions students or student problems. Perhaps the reason is similar to the reason that development officers rarely mention financial matters and fund raising as sources of frustration: They view such problems as part of their job.

The chief sources of frustration among student affairs officers are general administrative problems (mentioned by twenty-three of the forty-eight who were interviewed), personnel problems (mentioned by sixteen), the faculty (mentioned by ten). In addition, seven say they are frustrated by not having enough time. Five also mention the president as a source of frustration, although none of the other vice-presidential officers view the president in this light. Perhaps this slight animosity reflects student affairs officers' not-quite-equal status among top administrators.

Also unique to the student affairs officers is the feeling that the general conservatism of the institution constitutes a block; this theme runs throughout many of their comments:

- I and the president face the problem of chief officers who remain from the previous presidency and who don't want year-round operations, equal opportunity, coeducation.
- The Educational Policy Committee, influenced by faculty opposition, refused to have mini-courses listed on student transcripts.
- The faculty in general is resistant to change.
- The financial posture of the institution will not permit changes to take place as rapidly as I want; it's really frustrating.
- [I am most frustrated by] anyone who is resistant to change because it is change, anyone who instinctively relates to a new idea with suspicion.

Asked what they would do differently if they had it to do over again, student affairs officers—like the other vice-presidents —are most likely to say that they would handle certain administrative matters differently (mentioned by sixteen). Ten say they would handle personnel matters differently, five mention matters related to faculty, five mention matters related to students, five say they would do nothing differently, and five say they would not have taken the job in the first place.

On the whole, student affairs officers are the high-level administrators most deeply concerned with students and involved in the daily life of the campus. Nonetheless, they manifest considerable discontent with their jobs, particularly with their own status and influence. Decisions involving student discipline are particularly painful for them, and they are irritated by the general conservatism of their administrative and academic colleagues.

### Registrars

The sample of registrars includes a larger proportion of women than any other group of administrators surveyed: Of the forty-two who completed questionnaires, twenty-seven are female. Registrars are the second oldest group, after fiscal officers; their mean age is forty-eight years. They have been at their institutions longer than any other group (for a mean of fifteen years). Only 8 percent have the doctorate, although over one quarter have taught undergraduates in the three years prior to the survey.

The traits they most value in their subordinates are effectiveness in working with students, cooperation, initiative, professional or technical competence, and interpersonal skills; in all these values, they resemble student affairs officers. Unlike the latter, however, they do not ask that their subordinates be creative or take risks; they also tend to put less emphasis on salesmanship and frankness than do other groups of administrators. They are second only to academic officers in wanting their subordinates to have faculty support and value competitiveness and influence with those in power more than any other group of administrators.

The registrars present a mixed picture with respect to job satisfaction. More than three fourths say they are very satisfied with the challenge and responsibility of their jobs and with the congeniality of their coworkers. A majority also report satisfaction with their autonomy in decision making, task variety, competence of their coworkers, and relations with students. In short, they seem fairly happy with the actual duties of the office and the work environment. Moreover, three in five rate their job security as high, consistent with their relatively long tenure at their colleges.

Registrars are more likely than any other group of administrators to be very satisfied with their opportunities for scholarly pursuits and with the time they have for family and for leisure activities. Registrars seem to have less demanding jobs—with more regular hours and fewer travel requirements—than do other groups of administrators. Moreover, more than half the registrars are very satisfied with fringe benefits. But only one in five is very satisfied with salary, making them the second most unhappy group (after financial aid officers) in this regard. Their discontent seems to be justified; surveys show that registrars' salaries are in the lower bracket among college administrators.

Moreover, registrars are less likely than any other group to express high satisfaction with their opportunities for advancement within the institution or for jobs at other institutions. According to Glennen and McCullough (1976), registrars—unlike middle managers in the private sector—have almost no upward mobility. The registrars in our sample also tend to be dissatisfied with their personal status, power, and influence.

This last point is partly confirmed by the registrars' rather peripheral position in the communication network. Although they have personal contacts with students several times a day, with faculty almost daily, and with academic officers such as deans several times a week, they are rather isolated from other administrators, especially the president and the fiscal officer. About three fourths rely frequently on personal conversations to learn about other areas of administration (a lower proportion than for most other groups), and slightly over half depend frequently on meetings. They are more likely than are most other groups of administrators to make frequent use of newsletters, the student newspaper, and faculty members. One in four say that gossip, hearsay, and the grapevine are frequent sources of information, and 45 percent rely on this mode occasionally.

The responses of registrars to the open-ended interview question "Who or what inhibits you, frustrates you, or opposes you within your institution?" are so varied as to be difficult to classify. Some mention very specific problems such as the data-processing center: "The computer. . . . There's more they can't do than they can do." The complaints of others are more general: for example, the amount of paperwork and the scarcity of time for long-range management. The faculty is a source of frustration for some; registrars cite the difficulties of getting information from faculty, and the faculty's lack of knowledge about the registrar's office.

Asked what they would do differently if they had it all to do again, some registrars say there is nothing they would change, others would never have accepted the job. Some cite the need for better preparation: courses in statistics or longer internships.

When asked during the interviews whether they feel that they have adequate input into the administration of the college, registrars give mixed responses that can be divided into three distinct categories. The first are clearly positive: Seven of the sixteen registrars interviewed mention that they have voting rights or that they participate in major governing bodies or councils of the college. Three registrars give clearly negative answers, saying that they have no input, that they are treated like "second-rate administrators" or "hired help" rather than like decision makers. The third group (six registrars) acknowledge that their input is either minimal or nonexistent but seem untroubled by this fact.

In summary, registrars occupy a somewhat peripheral position among administrators; they perceive their status to be low, although some express satisfaction with this state of affairs. Perhaps their lack of influence and their low salaries are balanced, to some degree, by their having more free time. Generally they seem to feel that they are in dead-end jobs with few opportunities for advancement, a perception supported by their relatively long tenure at their institution.

### Admissions Officers

Admissions officers are the youngest group of administrators, averaging thirty-nine years of age. Of the forty who completed questionnaires, twelve are women. Only one in ten has the doctorate, and a mere 3 percent (the lowest proportion of any group of administrators) have taught undergraduates within the three years prior to the survey.

The most valued traits among subordinates, mentioned by at least 90 percent, are effectiveness in dealing with students, professional or technical competence, initiative, and interpersonal skills. Admissions officers are also more likely than are most other groups of administrators to name willingness to accept authority, frankness, and salesmanship as desirable traits for subordinates to have.

Admissions officers at some institutions occupy more prestigious positions than their title indicates (on this point, see Chapter Two). Thus, it is not surprising to find that they express considerable satisfaction with their jobs, much more so than do registrars or financial aid officers. They are second only to presidents in giving high ratings to the variety of their tasks and their visibility for jobs at other institutions. Satisfaction with the challenge and responsibility of their jobs is reported by 85 percent, and more than half are happy with their personal status, autonomy, power, and influence. Their relations with students and with coworkers are also good. But only a relatively small proportion think very highly of the competence of their colleagues.

Admissions officers express less satisfaction with their salaries, opportunities for advancement within their own institutions, fringe benefits, and job security. Only 5 percent (the smallest proportion of any group of administrators except presidents) say that they have enough time for scholarly pursuits.

Not surprisingly, given the nature of their jobs, admissions officers are far more likely than other administrators to have frequent contacts with potential students, seeing them several times a day. Other frequent contacts involve students, the financial aid officer, the registrar, and visitors. In all likelihood, visitors, whom admissions officers contact even more often than do presidents or development officers, often include prospective students and their parents. Unlike the other middle managers, they have fairly frequent contact with the president as well as with the academic and fiscal officers. They also rely more on personal conversation as a means of keeping informed about the administration than do the other middle managers. The next most frequently used sources of information are meetings (though these are less important than for most other administrators), memoranda, and formal reports. One quarter rely on newsletters frequently, and one half occasionally. Like registrars, admissions officers often depend on gossip as an information source: 25 percent use it frequently, and 45 percent occasionally.

Despite their relatively high status and general satisfaction, admissions officers nonetheless encounter some frustrations in their jobs. Of the seventeen who were interviewed, eight name specific administrative offices or officers as a source of frustration, six mention general administrative problems (including public relations), and five specifically mention not having enough time and being interrupted too often. Finally, like development officers, some admissions officers are inclined to chafe at the slow pace of academic governance: "The present structure is cumbersome. Not enough coordination, cooperation, or mutual helping."

Asked how they cope with frustrations, more than three quarters mention some specific action that they take to minimize or head off irritations:

- I set aside time each week for a staff meeting; we assess weekly objectives to manage better.
- If sufficiently convinced that a project is worthwhile, I do it catch-as-catch-can. Then I present the fact that we tried it on an experimental basis, it has worked: please give us some support.
- You have to make people aware of overall institutional goals and policies as compared to department policies.

Other admissions officers use escape behavior or indulge in hobbies as a means of coping with frustrations; some give stoic responses to this question: "grit my teeth and bear it," or "try to ignore it."

Asked what they would do differently, ten of the seventeen interviewees give specific practical answers:

- [I would develop] closer relationships with top administration in early years; deal better with everyday needs and larger office problems; get at the big things and leave the nitty-gritty.
- I wouldn't have plunged into work so fast. I would have taken time to introduce myself to everybody in the college; it was very busy and frantic when I came.
- I would change a lot of small things in terms of operations.

Five say they would handle staffing matters differently, and others give miscellaneous responses: "I would have left about four years ago. There's no upward mobility here. And I would have been more serious about working on my Ph.D."; and "I'd make myself a different person . . . warmer and friendlier."

The responses of admissions officers to the question of whether they have adequate input into the administration fall into three categories: strongly positive, positive with qualifications, and negative. In the first category are the following comments:

- Yes. We have easy access to the president and academic vice-president. They listen and seem to understand.
- Yes, because everyone is very interested in admissions, and I have an excellent relationship with my boss.

Those whose affirmative responses are qualified are represented by the following comments:

- I would say upward communications are the finest I've ever seen. It's not as good laterally as it is vertically.
- I have tremendous accessibility to anyone I want at the college. There's a difference between accessibility and effect. I don't feel that the vice-president for business should be able to overrule admissions.

Some negative comments are as follows:

• No. The new governance chart has pretty well screened out certain areas. I am not included at the decision-making level of the college. The Mount Olympus boys upstairs say we're represented through our vice-president, but development can't really speak for admissions. The president and the vice-presidents have their niche, the faculty and their committee theirs, but the middle-administrative level is excluded.
• No, because I don't sit on some policy-making bodies where I would provide some input.

To generalize, then, admissions officers are the most satisfied of the middle managers, although they do complain more than do registrars and financial aid officers of having too little time and too many interruptions. Such interruptions seem inherent to the nature of their jobs: Since they are primarily concerned with recruiting potential students, they must make themselves accessible at all times. Admissions officers are more likely than others to defuse their frustrations through hobbies or escape behavior. Asked what they would do differently, they are likely to name specific management strategies.

### Financial Aid Officers

Of the thirty-six financial aid officers who completed questionnaires, eleven are women. Their mean age is forty-two years, and they have been at their institutions an average of nine years. Only two have the doctorate, though six have taught undergraduates within the three years prior to the survey.

All of them say that effectiveness in dealing with students is a valuable trait for their subordinates to have. Other frequently mentioned traits are initiative, cooperation, professional or technical competence, and interpersonal skills. Financial aid officers are more likely than most other administrators (except fiscal officers) to place a premium on willingness to accept authority. They tend to give low ratings to creativity, they do not think it necessary that their subordinates have the support of faculty, and only two mention competitiveness as a desirable trait for subordinates.

Although more likely than any other group of administrators to say that they are very satisfied with their relations with students and with the competency of their colleagues, and although most find their jobs challenging and their relations with coworkers congenial, nonetheless financial aid officers are generally the most dissatisfied of all groups of administrators considered in this study. They are less likely than any other group to be very satisfied with their responsibility and variety in activities. Only 17 percent are very satisfied with their personal status, and only 19 percent with their opportunities for advancement within the college. Fewer financial aid officers than other administrators find their power, influence, and autonomy sufficient, and only 6 percent say they are very satisfied with their salaries.

Their lack of status, influence, and power is reflected in their patterns of communication. Although all of them see students several times a day and potential students several times a week, and although they have relatively frequent personal contacts with the admissions officer and the student affairs officer, they are less likely than other groups of administrators to be regularly in touch with the president, the academic officer, department chairs, or faculty; strangely, their contacts with their own staffs occur on the average of less than once a week.

Slightly more than two thirds frequently get information about other areas of the administration from personal conversations. They rely less than do other groups upon meetings and formal reports, and more on memoranda, the student newspaper, and the local press. Relatively few report that gossip or the faculty is a frequent source of information.

The comments made by financial aid officers during the interviews reflect their relatively low status. For instance, in response to the question about who or what at the institution inhibits or frustrates them, they are much more likely than others to mention staff shortages; one says that he does not even have a secretary. Perhaps the reason that financial aid officers have inadequate staff assistance is that others at the institution perceive them as disbursing money rather than acquiring it and are thus reluctant to furnish them with the necessary staff support.

Unlike registrars and admissions officers, they also have problems with students, particularly with students' carelessness in completing forms. Moreover, whereas registrars report being frustrated most by the faculty, and admissions officers say they are frustrated by people connected with student affairs, financial aid officers seem to be frustrated by a variety of administrators: the vice-president for student affairs, the vice-president for academic affairs, and the comptroller. Other financial aid officers mention general administrative problems not connected with any particular office or administrator: difficulty in obtaining information, inadequacy of resources, lack of focus in administrative responsibility, and inability to fulfill student expectations.

In coping with frustrations, financial aid officers are most likely to take specific measures that involve improving human relations: "I try to create a humane working situation by making people feel their job is probably the most important one in my entire operation."

Asked what they would do differently if they had things to do over again, many of the financial aid officers mention financial matters:

• I would try to find other sources of aid. I could research the possibilities and maybe get some grants. I did so once, and I was so pleased.
• I would insist on budgeting two professional staff members, leading to a higher quality of operation. Our salaries in this office are not related to the quality of service we provide.

Only one of the financial aid officers interviewed gives a strongly affirmative answer to the question about having adequate input to the institution: "Very definitely. I have the best deal of anyone around. In the budget we have a very good working relationship." The majority give much more qualified answers: "I realize my job is subsidiary. It's not a high administrative office. I don't think I should have a tremendous input into the administration. I sometimes complain. We have an administrative committee, but [the institution] has this team, this small group that makes most of the decisions." And some say flatly that they do not have adequate input: "We've been good boys at making do with what we have, but we don't have input in deriving the budget. With the need for accountability, we need to have more input into decision making"; and "Probably not. I think there are implications that we have for recruitment and retention which are not sought but which have to be offered."

In short, financial aid officers seem to have lower status than any other group of administrators considered in this study. They are more dissatisfied with their jobs than others, they seem to be more isolated from the higher echelons of administration, and they encounter many problems that other middle managers do not have, specifically staff shortages and difficulties with students. In dealing with their frustrations, they are more likely than others to rely on improving human relations; this too may reflect their lack of power and influence and their inability to impose their wishes on others.

# References

American Association for Higher Education and the National Education Association. Task Force on Faculty Representation and Academic Negotiations. *Faculty Participation in Academic Governance.* Washington, D.C.: American Association for Higher Education and the National Education Association, 1967.

"Administrators' Salaries in Academe—1978–1979." *Chronicle of Higher Education*, April 9, 1979, p. 6.

Argyris, C. *Understanding Organizational Behavior.* Homewood, Ill.: Dorsey Press, 1960.

Astin, A. W. *The College Environment.* Washington, D.C.: American Council on Education, 1968.

Astin, A. W. *Preventing Students from Dropping Out.* San Francisco: Jossey-Bass, 1975.

Astin, A. W. "Academic Administration: The Hard Core of Sexism in Academe." *UCLA Educator*, 1977a, *19* (3), 60–66.

Astin, A. W. *Four Critical Years: Effects of College on Beliefs, Attitudes, and Knowledge.* San Francisco: Jossey-Bass, 1977b.

**229**

Astin, A. W., Bowen, H. R., and Chambers, C. M. *Evaluating Educational Quality*. Washington, D.C.: Council on Postsecondary Accreditation, 1979.

Astin, A. W., and Henson, J. W. "New Measures of College Selectivity." *Research in Higher Education*, 1977, *6* (1), 1–9.

Astin, A. W., and Lee, C. B. T. *The Invisible Colleges: A Profile of Small Private Colleges with Limited Resources*. New York: McGraw-Hill, 1971.

Astin, A. W., and Panos, R. J. *The Educational and Vocational Development of College Students*. Washington, D.C.: American Council on Education, 1969.

Baird, L. L., Hartnett, R. T., and Associates. *Understanding Student and Faculty Life: Using Campus Surveys to Improve Academic Decision-Making*. San Francisco: Jossey-Bass, 1980.

Baldridge, J. V., and Tierney, M. *New Approaches to Management: Creating Practical Systems of Management Information and Management by Objectives*. San Francisco: Jossey-Bass, 1979.

Baldridge, J. V., and others. "The Impact of Institutional Size and Complexity on Faculty Autonomy." *The Journal of Higher Education*, 1973, *44* (7), 532–547.

Baldridge, J. V., and others. *Policy Making and Effective Leadership: A National Study of Academic Management*. San Francisco: Jossey-Bass, 1978.

Blau, P. M. *The Organization of Academic Work*. New York: Wiley, 1973.

Bowen, H. R., and Minter, W. J. *Private Higher Education: Second Annual Report on Financial and Educational Trends in the Private Sector of American Higher Education*. Washington, D.C.: Association of American Colleges, 1976.

Cass, J., and Birnbaum, M. *Comparative Guide to American Colleges*. New York: Harper & Row, 1973.

Clark, B. R. *The Distinctive College: Antioch, Reed and Swarthmore*. Chicago: Aldine, 1970.

Clark, B. R. "Belief and Loyalty in College Organization." *The Journal of Higher Education*, 1971, *42* (6), 499–515.

Cohen, M. D., and March, J. G. *Leadership and Ambiguity: The American College President.* New York: McGraw-Hill, 1974.

Drucker, P. F. *The New Society.* New York: Harper & Row, 1950.

Drucker, P. F. *Management Tasks, Responsibilities, Practices.* New York: Harper & Row, 1974.

Educational Facilities Laboratory. *The Neglected Majority: Facilities for Commuting Students.* New York: Academy for Educational Development, 1977.

Etzioni, A. *Modern Organizations.* Englewood Cliffs, N.J.: Prentice-Hall, 1964.

Glennen, R. E., and McCullough, J. B. "Selection Trends in College Administrative Positions." *Education,* 1976, *96* (4), 384–387.

Goodman, P. *The Community of Scholars.* New York: Random House, 1962.

Gullick, L. H., and Urwick, L. (Eds.). *Papers on the Science of Administration.* New York: Institution of Public Administration, Columbia University, 1937.

Haire, M. *Psychology in Management.* (2nd ed.) New York: McGraw-Hill, 1964.

Hammond Incorporated. *World Atlas.* Maplewood, N.J.: Hammond, 1974.

Herzberg, F., Mausner, B., and Snyderman, B. B. *The Motivation to Work.* New York: Wiley, 1959.

Hodgkinson, H. L. "Presidents and Campus Governance: A Research Profile." *Educational Record,* 1970, *51*, 159–166.

Kauffman, J. J. "Presidential Assessment and Development." In C. F. Fisher (Ed.), *New Directions for Higher Education: Developing and Evaluating Administrative Leadership,* no. 22. San Francisco: Jossey-Bass, 1978.

Lovejoy, C. E. *Lovejoy's College Guide.* (12th ed.) New York: Harper & Row, 1976.

McGregor, D. *The Human Side of Enterprise.* New York: McGraw-Hill, 1960.

March, J. G., and Simon, H. A. *Organizations.* New York: Wiley, 1958.

Maslow, A. H. *Motivation and Personality*. New York: Harper & Row, 1954.

Millett, J. *The Academic Community*. New York: McGraw-Hill, 1962.

Peterson, W. D. "Critical Incidents for New and Experienced College and University Presidents." *Research in Higher Education*, 1975, *3*, 45–50.

Sanders, I. T. "The University as a Community." In J. A. Perkins (Ed.), *The University as an Organization*. New York: McGraw-Hill, 1973.

Scott, R. A. *Lords, Squires, and Yeomen: Collegiate Middle Managers and Their Organizations*. AAHE-ERIC/Higher Education Research Report No. 7. Washington, D.C.: American Association for Higher Education, 1978.

Stroup, H. *Bureaucracy in Higher Education*. New York: Free Press, 1966.

Taylor, F. W. *The Principles of Scientific Management*. New York: Harper & Row, 1912.

Weber, M. *The Theory of Social and Economic Organization*. New York: Free Press, 1947.

# Index